Advance Praise for *Head*

T0009672

"An intimate and layered portrait of
—*Kirkus Reviews* (starred review)

"*Head above Water* is a rare feat: a lyrical, magnificently intelligent chronicle of what it's like to be a woman creating a life in literature while also disabled by the fragmentations of multiple sclerosis. Shahd Alshammari is remarkably attuned to what it feels like when your body, the home for every experience you will ever have on this earth, is painfully, severely, irrevocably disrupted by the colonial forces of an often-misunderstood illness."
—**Anita Felicelli, author of *Chimerica: A Novel***

"A kaleidoscopic and revelatory account of living with illness in an ableist world. With originality and honesty, Alshammari circles the question of what a good life looks like with illness. It is a story of living with limitations and restrictions, in particular those imposed on the stories expected of Arab women, and how a love of literature can help us navigate the world. The author articulates the power of the relationship between teacher and student, and what can still be revealed to those closest to us when we return to the past."
—**Alice Hattrick, author of *Ill Feelings***

"Shahd Alshammari's memoir of life with MS is one of the first distinctly twenty-first-century illness narratives. She situates chronic illness at the intersection of issues that include gender, exile, medical experimentation, and the politics of the Middle East. Her memoir becomes truly a dialogue, as her story fills with the voices of other women and men she has known, and how illness disrupted their lives."
—**Arthur W. Frank, author of**
The Wounded Storyteller: Body, Illness, and Ethics

"Shahd Alshammari's sensuous prose explores the manipulation of memory, the question of time, and gender politics. We are invited to reconsider the intricacies of love, the body, motherhood, the pervasive power of language, the power of women's education, and the synergy between the professor and the student."

—**Jokha Alharthi, author of** *Celestial Bodies: A Novel*

"A tale that will resonate with far too many readers, of someone told far too early by far too many people that their body—its femininity, its autoimmunity, its non-whiteness, its origins outside of western culture—will fail, is already beyond hope, and will never, ever, be good enough. It's a crushing experience that almost everyone has had, but Alshammari's steady and thoughtful voice lets readers feel buoyed, held, resilient—even triumphant."

—**Anne Elizabeth Moore, author of**
Body Horror: Capitalism, Fear, Misogyny, Jokes

"Shahd Alshammari's *Head above Water* is a tour de force. The memoir is an exchange between teacher and student and so it's in lineage with Socrates. 'Be brave. Be willing to lose people for a dream,' Alshammari writes. Brilliant."

—**The Cyborg Jillian Weise,**
author of *The Book of Goodbyes: Poems*

"A welcome addition to the growing body of illness narratives. Alshammari conveys eloquently and candidly the randomness of her multiple sclerosis, communicating what it's like to live in her body—Arab, female, disabled—and how her illness has shaped her education and her life as an academic. Her prose is at once lively and deadly serious, vividly somatic and deeply thoughtful, and highly engaging. Her book succeeds at a difficult endeavor: narrating chronic illness without imposing a false narrative arc on that experience."

—**G. T. Couser, author of** *Recovering Bodies:*
Illness, Disability, and Life Writing

HEAD ABOVE WATER

REFLECTIONS ON ILLNESS

SHAHD ALSHAMMARI

FOREWORD BY MARA MILLS

THE FEMINIST PRESS
AT THE CITY UNIVERSITY OF NEW YORK
NEW YORK CITY

Published in 2023 by the Feminist Press
at the City University of New York
The Graduate Center
365 Fifth Avenue, Suite 5406
New York, NY 10016

feministpress.org

First Feminist Press edition 2023

Originally published in the UK by Neem Tree Press Limited in 2022.

This is a work of creative nonfiction. It reflects the author's recollections of memories and experiences. Names and characteristics have been changed; some conversations have been recreated based on the author's flawed memory. Certain characters may be composites to protect the privacy of the people involved. The author has attempted to blend fiction with nonfiction while staying true to an illness narrative.

 This book was made possible thanks to a grant from the New York State Council on the Arts with the support of the Governor and the New York State Legislature.

First printing July 2023

Cover design by James Paul Jones
Text design by Drew Stevens

Library of Congress Cataloging-in-Publication Data
is available for this title.

ISBN 978-1-952177-07-1

PRINTED IN THE UNITED STATES OF AMERICA

For Mama,
who taught me how to read,
and pushed me to write.

"Trauma is rendered unspeakable because it is too dirty and dangerous, a filthy stray ghost dog scavenging on the margins, unfit to let into our house of words."

—Sophie Tamas

Contents

Foreword: Dislocations

May this book be contagious.

This warning and wish arrives in the final chapter of *Head above Water*, after the reader has spent hours immersed in the pages of Shahd Alshammari's book. *Head above Water* is one of the first disability memoirs from the Arab region, written from the perspective of a Palestinian-Bedouin woman living in Kuwait. A professor of English, Alshammari's previous books and articles have explored the limitations of Anglophone disability theory and Arabic literature alike with regard to the illness experiences of Arab women. "In Arabic literature," she writes, "discussions of the physically impaired female body are generally absent. They are also rare in Anglophone literatures or in literature written in English by Arab writers."[1] Working at this intersection, Alshammari never speaks "on behalf of the entire Arab world," as her graduate school professors in the UK asked her to do (120). *Head above Water* is written "from the body"—from Alshammari's distinct experiences with multiple sclerosis (MS) in far-flung national and social settings where ableism is a common denominator. In passages alternately addressed to a beloved former student and to the unknown reader, her insights about gender, ethnicity, and illness circulate via the contagion of disability pedagogy.

Head above Water is also remarkable in format—an alloy of diary, blog, conversation, and autobiography that expands the genre of life writing itself. It is the kind of text literary scholar Rebecca Sanchez and I have described as "crip authorship," noncompliant with regard to publishing conventions and spurring new methods and concepts through the creative force of disability.[2] Alshammari mentions gratefully coming across Virginia Woolf's essay "On Being Ill," with its early twentieth-century call for illness to be taken up as a central theme of future literature. Turning back to that article, we find that Woolf, too, recognized the compositional ingenuity of disability in the face of mis-fit and exclusion. "Let a sufferer try to describe a pain in his head to a doctor and language at once runs dry," Woolf writes. "There is nothing ready made for him. He is forced to coin words himself, and, taking his pain in one hand, and a lump of pure sound in the other . . . so to crush them together that a brand new word in the end drops out."[3] *Head above Water* is a book about pain, fatigue, trauma, and forgetfulness; the trembling of one's hand while holding a pen; the feeling that one has "failed language" (49). It is also a book that insists, in its form and content, that "illness is a place of exploration, a paradoxical place of loss and gain" (36).

One of the most startling formal innovations of the book relates to its organization. In a gesture that is equal parts aleatory and intimately collaborative, Alshammari allows her student Yasmeen, visiting her at home, to read through her diaries. Yasmeen remarks on certain passages: Alshammari's unbearable grief when her dog dies; the collision of racism and ableism when British strangers demand that she vacate a seat for disabled people on the bus; shame at being bathed by her mother or unable to zip her own pants. Yasmeen's moments of attention and concern become the pith around which chapters develop. The structure of *Head above Water* mirrors what Alshammari has called, here and in academic articles, the "random disability" of MS (27). A valuable contribution to the lexicon of disability studies, "random disability" encompasses temporary losses, recurrences, and disabilities that are otherwise unruly with regard to time. It's a theory precipitated out of the "multiplicity, vagueness" of MS (9).

In other passages, Alshammari theorizes dislocation across disability and migration. She has grown up thinking of exile as an ingrained condition. She recalls her grandmother's stories of fleeing an occupied Palestine, only allowed to carry one belonging, forced to throw her favorite doll over the side of the boat. When Alshammari's body itself becomes "unhomely" ("unheimlich"), when she can no longer recognize the taste of water or the sensation of wetness, she contemplates this physical estrangement as one node within her genealogy (62). She finds analogous traits in the phenomenon of speech impairment: a slur or a lisp from MS, a stutter when speaking in a non-native language.

A crucial intervention of *Head above Water* is its interrogation of certain ground truths in western disability studies. Alshammari has described her mode of writing as "autoethnography," a term coined by Mary Louise Pratt for "instances in which colonized subjects undertake to represent themselves in ways that engage with the colonizer's own terms."[4] Encountering illness narratives and disability theory during her graduate program in English literature, Alshammari reflects, "I didn't think of the body as separate from the mind, nor did I know anything about illness as metaphor" (8). She contests the individualism of the western rights-based model of disability, deflating its seeming universality. In her Bedouin father's tribe, disability is a collective matter, for better or for worse, a source of communal support as well as shared stigma (39). Disability scholar Ellen Samuels has argued that autotheory—a narrative practice and current publishing trend that braids theory and experience, or derives theory from the personal—too often "centers whiteness" and mines the lives of ill and disabled people for nondisabled revelations.[5] Alshammari autotheorizes otherwise, from a collective and "random" body, calling into question the "auto" that has been so celebrated in white women's writing.

Head above Water takes its title not from drowning but from buoyancy—the buoyancy of the disabled body. Alshammari leaves us in the littoral zone in the closing pages, nearshore, floating alongside her while the healthy wait on a fringe of sand. One of her final references is to the Emily Dickinson poem "Pain has an element of blank." The book itself is interspersed with blank pages, generous with margins and space—vacancies we are invited to occupy.

—Mara Mills
New York City
April 2023

Notes

1. Shahd Alshammari, "Writing an Illness Narrative and Negotiating Identity: A Kuwaiti Academic/Author's Journey," *Life Writing* 16, no. 3 (2019): 433.
2. In US disability studies, "crip" refers to cross-disability affiliation and disability justice activism. Mara Mills and Rebecca Sanchez, "On Crip Authorship and Disability as Method," in *Crip Authorship: Disability as Method*, eds. Mills and Sanchez (New York: New York University Press, 2023), 1–2.
3. Virginia Woolf, *On Being Ill with* Notes from Sick Rooms *by Julia Stephen* (Middletown, CT: Paris Press, 2012), 7.
4. Mary Louise Pratt, *Imperial Eyes: Travel Writing and Transculturation* (London: Routledge, 1992), 7. See also Shahd Alshammari, "On Being Woman, Other and Disabled: Navigating Identity," *Word and Text: A Journal of Literary Studies and Linguistics* 8 (2018): 37–47.
5. Ellen Samuels, "Twenty-Seven Ways of Looking at Crip Autotheory," in *Crip Authorship: Disability as Method*, eds. Mara Mills and Rebecca Sanchez (New York: New York University Press, 2023), 205.

This work will oscillate between the present and the past. Scene breaks are used to help with the narrative's flow and the shifts in tense. As with the messiness of time and its illusions, one only needs to move along.

All I want is to wake up. I want to stay awake for this part of the story. If I manage to write, then I stayed awake. How to call upon my internal narrator to tell the story of a body, of a self that is trapped inside, yet completely convinced that there is no way out—except through the body? I am aware that time will have its say. I have perpetually sleepy eyes, and my eye muscles are closing in on me, bringing me disturbingly closer to myself. I have to close them. I have to look inside. What follows will be what comes through.

One

Chapter O of One

"You're very preoccupied with death, Professor. I've noticed."

I thought about this statement before responding to Yasmeen. She was one of my most brilliant students and had become my friend and confidante. I was not preoccupied with death as an ending. A visit to Death interrupted my life midway, at the age of twenty-five. I wonder sometimes if I can recall it as it happened, as I saw it, as I felt it, and the conversations I heard, the faces that I saw. Would I want to narrate this experience, tell the story (and stories) of this half-interrupted life? Stories are who we are. Stories make up our most vulnerable moments, and in storytelling we have the power to gain a sense of agency over our lives. In dialogue and in conversation are the moments that make sense of chaotic ruptures, fragments that we collect and reassemble to construct a grander narrative. I've always told my students that storytelling is an integral part of life. We cannot separate life from the stories we tell ourselves and others, the stories we tell ourselves about others, and stories others tell about us. But these stories are distorted by failing bodies, failing memories, and lapses, relapses, repeated delays in the transmission of brain signals to a body that forgets and remembers. Memory is a collection of snapshots in time, the work of remembering is hard labour, emotional at its best, traumatic at its worst. We can't help but project ourselves onto distorted mirrors, and pen and paper fail to convey what really happened, what was, and what wasn't.

How are we to tell the story from one perspective if we have never experienced the other? How can I speak as the mentor, when a student-self still pulsates in me? My characters are invoked from memories; at other times, accounts of others' jolts of memory, gaps that I can't seem to fill. Composite characters are part of this narrative, and what drives my recollection of emotions is the emotion behind intimate conversations, meditations, musings between myself, my mother and me, my grandmother's last words, my visions of our "human" life, and a preoccupation with these stories. Stories have been the pulse that allows me room to breathe around my ribcage as it pushes against my heart, threatening to suffocate it. My heart, our hearts, her heart, Mama's heart, all of their hearts—the place that the soul lives and dies in. Or, is it the place we turn to when we reflect on our lives? In the Quran, we are told about the vagueness of the soul and its home:

> *And they ask you about the soul. Say: The soul is one of the commands of my Lord, and you are not given aught of knowledge but a little. (17:85)*

And because souls are a vast area of the unknown, and we have limited and mortal knowledge, then the heart is the finding place, the knowing place. The mind, reason, thought, knowledge is the place where we ask the hows and whys and we find nothing but a road back into the heart. The method of the heart is my starting and ending point (and I don't promise an end). Binary thought will fail me as bodies fail to house us. I look at these bits and pieces as a bridge between that which I know to have happened, that which I think happened, and that which I fashion out of a big belief in narrating the self.

Some of these scenes are revisited through various diary entries and conversations. The question of the body will present itself as one of the big questions— whose body is it anyway? A vehicle in motion, a vehicle that stops, and then struggles to park itself, waiting for its rightful owner to smooth its tensions. Do these retellings and re-imagined truths bring us closer to a satisfactory conclusion, a process of meaning-making that will guide us through the woods? Literature has been my home for decades, and I want it to still be what I find at the end of the journey. The woods are darker than they seem, and I pause to think about Yasmeen's question. What is my fascination with death all about? Is there a meaning that we find in every grieving moment where the body falters, the mind freezes, and the soul stretches to find who it believes it really is?

Does time matter in the telling of these stories? Does gender stop us from speaking? The mute body must rise. The carcasses of our women, buried, fearing the dangers of being anti-heroic. Victims? Of? And, who's listening anyway?

"But Professor, voice is important. You said so yourself, in Theory class, remember?"

An interruption.

I can't say what I need to say, and I am not sure what needs to be said at this given moment in time. The personal is always political, I know Yasmeen will say it before her eyes say it. There is a blurry line and I choose to anchor myself here. Only here, where my head doesn't wobble. The tremors come and go, and I need to get to it.

I so often think back to education as a force in women's lives. Perhaps one way we come to be who we are goes back to the roots of education. Who taught us? Were they good teachers? Were they mentors both inside and outside the classroom? My grandmother, Sahar, was one of the first Palestinian teachers in Kuwait in 1949. After the occupation of Palestine, she fled the country with her siblings and recalls having to abandon her favourite ragged doll. Into the big ocean it went, drowning in its depths, an innocence that was never to be retrieved. That doll was her favourite, and her attachment to it was unbreakable. A bond that was not to be questioned. Except by war. It was no longer a question of survival. The doll had to go, and she chose to keep her high school certificate instead. *Only one item per person.* Only one object—and you really couldn't object to that.

Sahar had lost both of her parents. One was murdered and the other died of cancer. How, when, which year? Somewhere between 1948–1949. What matters is that she was orphaned and started teaching, when she was seventeen years old, Arabic to a group of girls in Kuwait. She was fluent in English and Arabic and was required to teach Arabic grammar and reading. It was a job that would pay the bills and women were deemed respectable if they were teachers. Fate had brought her to Kuwait, where she met her future husband. Aren't all stories always leading up to this moment in your narrative where you go from being a single woman to a married woman? Not for Sahar.

"I married him because that's what happens. You don't get to say no, if you have no reasons for it. I tried to say I wanted to teach for life, but teaching and marriage aren't counter opposites. Why not do both, they said." Sahar's voice comes back to me. I'm

6

listening to her, curled up in bed, as she tells me about love that comes to us after marriage.

"Professor, if we can love just about anyone, what does that say about us? Are we creatures of habit?" Yasmeen again.

I had asked my Tata the same question over twenty, thirty years ago. Is this ishra? If we continue living with the same person, does that routine become our understanding of the familiar, and of love? A repetition of events, as uncanny as they are, makes a solid event. It creates a sense of routine and a meaning. This was a time when women were still women and men had to be men. A time when partners had traditional gender roles to play, and no one threatened the status quo.

The love between Sahar and her husband grew with time and children. Each child bore a resemblance to one of them and cemented their pledge to one another. Greys in their hair added to the urgency of time. It's too late to leave. After all this time? Who would? When we fall out of love, we end up staying, and perhaps this is a time when you will question motives and speak of agency and integrity, but back then was a time of simplicity. Things were just the way they were, and you didn't need to question. The complexity lay in a darker place, in the body.

Sahar's body was heavy. In her sixties, she had a story to tell. She had given up her job as an educator, the one place she had found herself in, that classroom that made her feel alive and happy. She had had to leave Kuwait, along with thousands of Palestinians expelled after the Iraqi invasion. Twice expelled. Twice abandoned by a home. What was left was a body that carried the secrets of shame. Edward Said had said that exile is "strangely compelling to think about but terrible to experience." Tata thought about exile all the time. She felt it in her bones every day. She thought of her death every day.

"I want to be buried in Kuwait. My home. Make it happen. You are Kuwaiti and I know you can make it happen," she said to me. Wide-eyed and hopeful, I nodded diligently. Who could say no to Tata, her fierce Palestinian blood rising to her cheeks?

She wasn't buried in Kuwait, and there was no way she could have been. It's all sand at the end of the day and what happened before and after her death is what I carry with me.

Tata's fight with cancer made me think of the body as the container that we place our traumas in. I was an undergraduate student at the time and I didn't think of the body as separate from the mind, nor did I know anything about illness as metaphor, illness as symptom of the nation's decline, none of that stuff. I saw pain, and I linked pain to an immense loneliness, a pattern of sacrifice and loss that made no sense. I saw illness as a way for the heart to say, "I lost the battle." It was a war zone, and the heart had found its way into the woods, but not out of the woods. Tata was buried in the woods. I am sure many others were, too. At the time, all I saw was a body that had to go. What she took with her was her memory of teaching, her students' lives, and I thought about how that's all we exit stage with. In the same vein, I have her blood pulsating through me, a teacher's blood, the breath of language and literature and an understanding of home that has shifted throughout the years.

Chapter N of One

My toe glances over at my foot. I need to get up, open the door, where I know Yasmeen waits for me at the other side, anticipating as much as I am. She's come to help organise all these books. The books that I carried with me throughout all these years of studying, researching, and attempting to write. Only I know where each of these books sits. Do they really sit? They've always leaned against each other, in desperate need of a companion. I don't have a companion, other than Lucky, and she is sprawled comfortably on her couch-bed (the term Mama had given it). Lucky is a beautiful golden retriever, and before her, there was Flake who had been the greatest love I had known. Partly this was due to her understanding of pain. We both understood vulnerability and pain, her and arthritis, me and my debilitating disease. Multiple sclerosis (MS), only it sounded like multiplicity, vagueness, and it takes an obscure form that I can and cannot hide. Sometimes, days like this Saturday, I need my loud black cane, which announces itself with every thud. An extension, another part of me that feels too masculine. But I shouldn't care too much about that, given all the women's studies classes I have taught.

There is no denying my presence and its presence as I reach for the cane, silently, as quietly as possible so as to not disturb Lucky's slumber. I need the help getting around and I also need Yasmeen's help with organising my books. The Wise One, the Grasshopper, the Butterfly as I have nicknamed her in my mind, describing her qualities and budding personality. I have watched her grow into a literary scholar over the years and today she is working on a dissertation examining Judith Butler's theory of performativity and Arab female protagonists. She is here for the summer, and she had heard that I needed help. What she didn't know was just *how* much help.

"Professor! I missed you so much!" Yasmeen hugs me, as she often did in the past, warm, welcoming, open. Engulfed in her arms, I look up at her, realising yet again how tall she is, and how I must have shrunk even more since our last meeting.

And so, I talk, as she helps herself to the contents of my fridge. The fridge is blue because I had allowed my best friend Farida's beautiful baby girl, Dana, to paint all over it. Blue, the colour of possibility and endless hope. Infinite, as I thought back in the days when I was healthier and still reasoning I could pass through life unscathed, intact, and not robbed of dignity. Lately, I didn't feel like myself and I knew it was time to talk, especially because Yasmeen was always willing to listen. She had been that way in all of my classes, and now she was a friend whom I trusted. Mutual respect had developed over the years and we both confided in each other. She had come to me with her failed romances, her heartbreaks, and her inability to fit within a patriarchal society. She just couldn't stay home and was considering a job abroad. I had waited for her all these years, to come back to my university, to be my colleague, to teach next to me, side by side, literary comrades. And yet she was leaning more towards leaving the country and I didn't know whether to support her, let her go, or hold on to her.

There is a thin line between selfish love and pure love. Mama had said that. I looked over at Lucky and wondered whether there would be a time to let her go too. Not yet, not yet. There's always more time.

"I've been thinking that you should write another book. Maybe I could help you?" Yasmeen suggests, looking at me with curious and hopeful eyes.

I can't seem to find a character; I can't seem to find the time. Or the clarity. I am forgetting almost everything that I ever saw, felt, touched. I am preoccupied with this body. I tell her this and look away, hoping that she won't ask for more.

But I had always pressed *her* for more. Elaborate, don't leave your reader hanging. There has to be a point to what you're trying to say even if the point is elusive. Find your way and take the reader along. You're a literary critic. But criticism had failed, and I was looking at life as random, meaningless. I couldn't tell her that because I believed I knew better. Even in meaninglessness there is meaning, a sense of a beginning and an ending. And there was a beginning, at some point, of my life, my disease, my first teaching days. That's where we had met after all. Life was a classroom and a handful of eager students.

"Professor, everything here is expired. I don't think you've opened your fridge in forever!" Yasmeen laughs. She has been here so many times over the past few years that I have lost count. When had this friendship formed? Perhaps it was at the very beginning of her graduate days. We used to sit together in my office, discussing books, protagonists (and to an extent, the seductiveness of antagonists). I watched as she acquired critical vocabulary and a voice that wasn't as breathless when she spoke. Wasn't it Hélène Cixous who had once urged us to watch when a woman speaks with her entire body, breathless, gasping for the words? She had been right. In every classroom, the smarter ones choked. Sometimes I did too, but I had gotten better at hiding it. Age is an armour to wear when confronted with any demons.

Lucky and Yasmeen look at each other. The beauty of friendship between two generations, two species, two worlds apart. Yasmeen is a younger version of me, and, as so many of my colleagues had noticed, a stronger and gentler one. Comfortable in her body, in her skin. In a society that demanded children from women before the age of thirty, she had made her choices.

Throughout every conversation we had shared, both of us had learned a bit more about vulnerability, love, pain, and life. These bits of conversations started again when Yasmeen asked me to write.

"I found a note you wrote to me when I graduated. Do you remember, you used to give your students notes to remind them of who they were? Mine said: *Be brave. Be willing to lose people for a dream.* And it was so simple. But I remember the line."

I do, too.

"So, what do you have to lose now, if you were to write a second book?" she parries.

I've already lost parts of my body and the people I'm writing about are ghosts. Some never existed. I want to create another me.

"Could she/he be a professor, too? It's a big part of who you are."

Characters are more than just their jobs. They're more than just their names. What makes a soul any different from another's? What is in a name? I had spent a finite number of years learning my students' names. 182 per semester. I thought of it as a game. I would say each name silently, then under my breath, and finally out loud. I would smile, hoping to soften the blow if it was the wrong name. Practicing their names helped me exercise my memory. At the time, I still believed you could control the outcome. The progression could slow down. Like an hourglass, my body twisted and turned into itself to escape time.

But then I turned to stories and my novels. To Arab and women writers. To memoir and to fiction. To Disability and to Gender. What story to write when there was so much to tell—and so very little space to capture it in? Space. The psychic space, not the pages, not their feel against my hands, which I think I remember were dry. Today, sensation is not part of life and the physical texture of objects is no longer tangible, it is only in the distant memory of what they once felt like. Objects carry their descriptive and prescriptive qualities, filed somewhere between the neurons and the scar tissue in my brain. Paper has a distinct feeling to it, just like all the stories of the women who'd crossed over. They crossed into territory that you dreamed up, made up, and sometimes came so close to. This was the other world—the place you visited once and from where had never been able to Return. This was the place I had died in and what I thought I heard and saw. What I tasted.

"Give yourself some time. You always used to say, take your time. You owe the world nothing more than to take your time. I'm here for a month and meanwhile I'll arrange these books and all of these—notebooks? I'll come once a week." Yasmeen points to stacks of black, leather-bound notebooks.

My diaries, journal entries from years ago. I don't remember.

She suggests typing them up. It would be nice to have them somewhere, if only for me to read, or others, she jokes. Who else would want to read them? I had kept a blog throughout the years, too. But the blog was more for the public, and I had constructed it in a way where the narrative was clearer. My diary entries are jolts of criticisms, questions, and moments where I thought I couldn't move.

Yasmeen can type up these entries if she can read my handwriting. Tremors never let me finish a sentence without traumatising the pen, any pen. I had trained my left hand to write, but it could never do a good job. Lately, neither of my hands are doing the job I imagine they had once been able to do. I remember the first time I got introduced to the usage of rubber bands, not for papers, but for working out which finger belongs to which hand. It has been years since I last visited Alex, the physiotherapist and Pilates instructor who introduced the importance of working with the body's strength in order to build resistance. "A strong core," she used to say. The core. That series of muscles that hold all of you up together. When she had explained how the spine is the most important part of our bodies, I questioned whether this included how we felt about our bodies. My spine was made up of all the stories I carried with me, the ones I had read, taught, and listened to.

Yasmeen is now leafing through the journals and has brought over a glass of iced tea. Everything cold soothes the prickling heat I feel on my skin and no matter how I am used to Kuwait's burning summer temperatures, I still struggle with skin that retaliates against imaginary attacks. We start by discussing her thesis and how she's been feeling lately. I wonder if she's struggling with anxiety again and she assures me that it's been some time since she last panicked about her studies. She's come a long way. So many students had dealt with anxiety attacks throughout school and so many had experimented with medication, sometimes as the first resort, without ever committing to therapy. This was an epidemic that I couldn't wrap my head around. What was happening to this generation of young students who struggled with examinations, deadlines, and panicked upon being asked to comment during the discussion? There was a lot of talk about anxiety and panic and how to self-heal, self-talk, and of course, the unbelievable amount of prescriptions. Most students had wanted to jump to the last stage. Anyone who had the authority to prescribe medication and didn't take too long talking to people was the most popular. Over the years, I had listened to so many friends, students, colleagues, partners, ex-partners, speak of pain. So many of them had experimented with different ways to relieve the pain.

One theme kept emerging, but I wanted to write all the themes down while I still could. Or perhaps get someone else to write them down. Whatever the case, they were bound to be written. So many journals, so many notes, and there had to be a place for them. It didn't matter who would read them. Pain had to be exorcised. A huge part of my life had included carrying stories and wondering where they belonged. An even bigger part of me toyed with the possibility of what it may have been like for those who couldn't write or speak. Arthur Frank, the sociologist who wrote *The Wounded Storyteller*, had left his mark on me forever. Every wounded storyteller, marked one way or another, outcast, marginalised, had a lot to say. Stories are sometimes chaotic, sometimes linear, and sometimes, there is hardly a story. But the feeling remains.

And this is what I wanted to tell Yasmeen, that even if I wrote these stories, they wouldn't solve anything, they wouldn't make any difference in the grand scheme of things. But they would grasp the emotion at the heart of the narrative—the feeling carried within the bones of the souls that shared their stories. Capture the emotion, narrate it, transfer it. Feel it.

"I have an idea. I will come to you with a few questions tomorrow and then these questions can be the starting point. That's a plan, right?" Yasmeen asks holding one of my favourite books in her hands. *The God of Small Things*.

I remember how Arundhati Roy began that book . . . "However, for practical purposes, in a hopelessly practical world . . . "

And that's how this book emerges. For practical purposes, bits of a diary entry precede conversations. And conversations invoke memories. Memories stem from stories or perhaps it's the other way around. Stories I carry within my body have worked their way through my memories and I can't tell which ones are mine, and which have seeped in from the outside.

Chapter E of One

Diary Entry: "I am struggling with the flu and I am struggling to accept my dog's impending death—Flake. Even as I write the word death and her name, Flake, in one sentence, I cringe. I'm giving it meaning when it just feels so distant. Flake will be euthanised on Saturday. I have come to the decision after endless suffering for both of us. I am terrified of loss and how empty the world will feel without her. I am terrified of crying; I am terrified of not being strong enough. I grew up under a strong Palestinian mother, and you know what they say about Palestinians. They are the products of exile, war, dislocation. They are survivors of trauma and they carry that in their genes. I don't think this is a myth."

Yasmeen reads this diary entry out loud. She wants to talk about death and she has started where it hurts the most. The wound that still bleeds.

"Since you're so preoccupied with death, I broke it down into thinking about deaths of companions and selves."

Death, Yasmeen, is, if you remember, the hardest theme to explore. We spoke about it all the time in class. I don't think there's a novel that I ever taught that didn't have characters tragically dying. But it's that one theme where we end up thinking it's all done with. Death is a state of paralysis, it's not an ending in itself. It stops us from moving. They talk to us about moving on, but we can't think past that moment of paralysis. Of losing a limb. Right now, I can't feel my legs.

Technically, they're dead, by the logic of my neurologist. And science. Science knows it all, they tell all of us humanities majors. I haven't ever seen a case where pure science made sense. A little bit of magic, a little bit of imagination, a little bit of faith in words. That's how even death becomes an interruption. There's so much to say about death, and I'm not sure I can talk about it without thinking of loss and love. We think of grief as this stage that passes, but we also think of it as reserved solely for our human companions. Our lovers. Our family. For many people like me, we live alone. Disability has always been a part of my life, as far back as I can remember. Companionship isn't as easy when your body fails you. I am not generalising, and I know you know there are different types of disabilities, physical, mental, and invisible. What I do know about disability is that so many times it leaves people isolated. It left me isolated for the longest time because I could not translate pain. I couldn't put it into words for any of my able-bodied partners. And they always left. Sometimes, it was me who ended up leaving. It was like we existed on two separate planes. We experience the world through our bodies and what we see, touch, hear—think of all your senses. I've always thought of the body as a vehicle.

What made my relationship with Flake different was how there was this silent understanding of life as moments and of pain as part of these moments. We grow old. It is inevitable. When Flake started growing older, her breath changed, her limbs grew thinner, her paws grew softer. I could see death come for her in flashes. Episodes. We lived together for fifteen years, day in and day out. She shared my bed. And there's a bond there that is hard to explain for those who haven't lived with a dog. Your bodies synchronise in a bizarre way. Her snoring meshed with mine and at times I wasn't sure if my snoring bothered her or soothed her. It was a state of presence. The bed was never empty.

When Flake's time was ticking down, I was terrified. There was no way I could imagine that it was me who had to make a choice to let her go. She was in a lot of pain. And I wanted to hold on, to keep her, to immortalise her, but Tamara, my good friend, the vet, urged me to think about quality of life. And who could understand quality of life other than me—someone who has endured pain over the years and has often thought about how much easier it would be for me to just exit this stage? I loved Flake. I knew she could barely walk without the excruciating pain she felt and I saw it in her eyes. There was no language needed for that. Sometimes language fails and, in her case, I felt no language could capture what we both felt. Silence is loud, my Mama used to say.

And Mama was part of the reason I couldn't cry. I couldn't cry for days before Flake's euthanising. I finally cried when I held her in my arms as Tamara injected her with the solution that would end her pain. The solution to it all. Her life. Her journey with me. My journey with her. I rocked her back and forth in my arms, kissed her white whiskers, and said, "Goodnight, baby girl. Goodnight." I remember the way her eyelids drooped and she closed her eyes, taking one last breath. And that one last breath was all I needed to stop being terrified of crying. Death. A word so heavy and a word I cannot hear. It has a melody to it even with its heaviness. As she took her last breath, death entered the picture and stayed with me. How ironic is it that breath and death rhyme?

I was a mess of tears, a wreckage of human emotion

that had finally cracked open. With her death came an interruption of life for me, and a loss that I still can't explain. People told me "it's just a dog" and I stopped trying to defend that love. People always want to simplify death. It'll be over soon. You'll mourn for forty days, the azza is there to help you grieve (three days, and who's to say three days are ever enough?), and I keep asking myself, how do we quantify grief?

"How was your mother the reason behind you not crying?" Yasmeen's hazel eyes glowed.

Mama raised us to never cry. I can't say this worked with all of my sisters, but it certainly worked with me. We struggled to cry because crying was associated with victimisation. If you cried, you were likely to be seen as a girl. Weak. Someone who doesn't have it together. A tough life needs a tough core. If I cried all the time, I wouldn't be where I am today. But you can cry, and that's beautiful. It took me years of theory, reading, therapy, and thinking about vulnerability before I realised that crying was okay. We cry because we are strong enough to feel. We cry because we went through the woods and fell in love. We cry because we aren't always on autopilot. There is a beauty in allowing yourself to cry that I don't think many of us have mastered yet. I know that throughout the years I have been around women who aren't afraid to cry, but I have also seen women whose tears have dried up. They stopped crying. Maybe we stop crying when we have fallen down so many times, and each time we get right back up. Wobbly, yes, but there are moments when being your own crutch is a lot safer than breaking your own heart. We need to cry. I cried for days when Flake died, and I know I wondered about tears. How they don't stop even if you will them to stop. Remember how Alice's tears filled the hall? It was only when she was over nine feet tall that her tears overflowed. Because Alice was big, Yasmeen. Because she was big in her mind, in her heart, in her whole being, it was then that her tears had any value. It's part of the story. I was terrified of being big. I think I was always scared of that. Crying over a dog—over a lost part of my soul—meant that was a big deal. Everything that is big looms over us, and we either find ourselves enmeshed in it or reject it. Rejecting it kills, because the grief takes over. The pain expands and then you can't locate parts of you that existed before.

Two

Chapter T of Two

Diary Entry: "I am teaching my classes but I wonder if my neurologist was right. I was supposed to die by thirty. I'm still here. Was it a miscalculation?"

It's strange how compelling it is to think about your own death while you're still alive. I was eighteen years old when my neurologist told me that I would die early. MS doesn't kill anyone, but it took me years to understand that fact. I think you might find a few more entries on that, somewhere in the older notebooks.

○

I was an eighteen-year-old who fell asleep one random night and woke up the next day with complete numbness all over my body. The numbness crept up on me and settled in my skin. I slowly lifted myself up and scratched my skin, hoping that action would remind me that it was, in fact, mine. The skin reacted, but the feeling did not register in my head. I lingered in bed for a few days before my mother dragged me out and said that the room stank. It's intriguing how our environments mimic us. The room had lost its freshness, and I felt as though I was going to suffocate within the tight invisible bands wrapped around my arms and legs. My ribcage pushed against my heart, and in response to the beating it was getting, my heart retracted into my chest. Involuntarily, I would cough and shudder after the coughing fits. There was no explanation to what was happening to me.

"No more hiding in bed! You have to go to the hospital!" my mother screamed as she opened the windows to my room. As she did that, I knew there was no escaping. I had to drive myself to the hospital.

Driving while your body is no longer yours is a reckless act. I think back and wonder how I even managed, and what foolish thought had me believe I was immortal? What could I not see at the time? Did I not calculate the risks? Do our younger selves just think less, and by extension, worry less, care less? Was it a daring act or was I simply unaware of the consequences? I remember the roads being a blur as my head tried to absorb what was happening to me. The brakes under my feet were fluffy, like there was no hardness to them, no presence except that they claimed they were there.

Being so young and watching older people enter and exit the doctor's examination room felt odd. I was out of place, an imposter. This wasn't my place and I felt guilty as the others who were waiting for the doctor stared at me as if I had stolen something precious. It would take me years to understand that in fact, time with a medical doctor was precious. You want to be listened to and heard. Sometimes we aren't really looking for immediate solutions, only that your pain is valid. That it isn't all in your head. After being poked at, I was sent to neurology. It seemed I was under an attack from something within my brain.

I was sent for an MRI and the results proved inflammatory cells were attacking other "good cells" in my body for an unknown reason. Science couldn't explain it. The body was making too much of something. The body was in hyper-reaction mode. The body was too aggressive. Too protective. Ready to attack. Burning itself away. Like a candle, working so hard, lighting the way, and burning itself in the process. I thought of my cells as a confused army that committed suicide because it was all too draining, too difficult. It was the trauma of war that made the soldiers fire at themselves. It was over.

The neurologist who read my results frowned and paused for what felt like hours—although I am sure it must have been seconds—before delivering the fatal blow. There was no way out of it, I was definitely going to be bedridden within ten years, he said. This was an incurable disease, one that couldn't make sense even if he tried to explain it to me in simple terms. He didn't even voice the name of the disease as he sat there shaking his head. All he could say was to make good use of time, while I could still function. I still had a few years to go, but given how violent the war in my brain was, I couldn't expect survival as an outcome. "Insha'Allah it will be okay," he kept repeating. Insha'Allah. If God wills. Only if God wills it will be okay.

Collateral damage, I thought. Which parts of me would remain in a few years? Would it be my senses that remained? Which senses? Was hearing more important than sight? What about smell? Touch? Which was more important to everyday life?

It would be random, there was no telling. "No two cases are the same," he had explained.

And to be fair, this randomness is what I ended up embracing over the years. Living in this body is a state of randomness. I've termed it as "random disability" in one of my academic papers. I forget which one, and it doesn't matter. What I had meant was that I would and should expect to randomly lose parts of me and my senses. It didn't feel like a full disability because there were many days where I looked and felt healthy. You wouldn't have ever guessed. But this isn't just about disability. What really matters is if we can actually think of life as random, and not in a cliché and theoretical way. It is random. There's a lot to think about when you open your eyes and wonder if your fingers and toes still move. If you can actually brush your teeth in the morning or need to come up with a different way to do the same task. There's a lot at stake. I can't say it's easy to accept that life is random and that every day is not simply "another day," but a day that stands on its own. I can't see life as one moment that leads to another. It's a lot more disjointed. One moment you're disabled, the next you're fine. One moment your vision is superb, and the next you're batting your eyelashes frantically, wishing that the dust specks would go away. But nothing goes away unless it wants to. You can't wish it away. But there are exceptions to every rule. I think I was the exception to my neurologist's prediction. Let's call him Dr. S for the sake of anonymity, for the sake of making him shrink in my head. See, in my memory he's a dark and looming figure, the kind that towers above you. And he's the type that doesn't ask if he can touch your feet. He's the type that shames you under his gaze for not shaving your legs. Like holding a blade to your skin was the polite thing to do.

When you're young and still very much aware of your body, with its breasts, its curves, its indentations, its markers as a body that needs to be covered, you end up really aware of the places it occupies. How you move and manoeuvre it, and how much attention it demands. Women's bodies are different and of course, I know that disabled bodies are in general stared at and made to feel inferior. But think of how many women feel ashamed for being women. How many women fear rejection? How many small deaths happen every day as we continue feeling less desirable? Bodies are strange, I tell you, Yasmeen. Bodies make me think of souls, and I sometimes question whether the soul ever got as much attention as the body. Bodies demand and maintain our attention. Souls nudge us but don't steal the limelight. You can't deny what you see; it's right there. Lying across the white bed as the doctor asked me to stretch my legs, curl my toes, feel the unfamiliar sensations of every tool he used—I felt as though I had shamed my father and everyone who had ever loved me. I just wanted to be invisibly ill, and I didn't want to be probed anymore. I was sorry I was causing so much trouble, taking up too much space, and demanding all this attention.

I liken this all-consuming feeling of shame to death. We say how much we wish the ground would eat us alive, how we want to evaporate, leave our bodies, leave existence. It's deep embarrassment, bone-felt shame that makes us wish we could die. It happens more often than we care to count. Back in the day, I grew up hearing stories of how women who shame the tribe can be killed. Cleansing the shame with blood was the only way it could vanish. The memory of the person would no longer be spoken of because they had died in blood, not a normal death, not a place of worthiness. Dying in your own blood would cleanse the tribe's shame because they were taking back what was rightfully theirs. Women's bodies were meant to be hidden or buried in the ground.

My body refused to be buried. It was screaming for attention and there was nothing I could do to stop its tantrum. Since I was a teenager, I was stuck bargaining with the doctors, asking them to give me room to stay alive. To not be buried as a number. I wanted them to see me, to give me answers. And because I needed to be seen and examined and studied, I felt I was taking up too much space in every hospital room I entered. I wanted to apologise constantly for causing so much disruption to my father's schedule. My father had been the person who took me with him to hospitals. Because he was a man, we saw doctors earlier than when I was alone. Doctors and nurses took me more seriously when my father introduced himself as a lawyer. I was just a teenager, a girl with long black hair tied up into a ponytail (because modesty was important, and long hair was too sexy). Hair had to be covered and if it wasn't covered, then it was best to hide it, to draw less attention to it. Each doctor I met glanced at me, afraid of locking eyes with me, unable to see the real me. There must have been a way for me to speak louder, but my voice was strained, barely audible. It makes me consider shame again—women's voices as taboo, as too tempting, "sot almara'a 'awra." So, my vocal cords refused to release. They remained nestled in my throat, staying out of men's earshot. My father spoke for me.

"What's wrong with her other than numbness?" the doctor asked.

"Nothing, she's as healthy as a horse," my dad replied, with a hint of pride in his eyes.

The doctor finally looked at me quizzically. There was no doubt that I had to say something now.

"I can't feel my face also. I can't close my eyes, it hurts. My tongue feels strange," I replied, barely able to look at either of the men.

He had to come really close to my face and I

could smell his breath on my cheeks and mouth. He touched my face and this was the first time a man's hands had roamed freely on me.

"It's not symmetrical, that's for sure. You woke up like this?"

"Yes—I think so," I replied, unsure about the word symmetrical. I hadn't looked in the mirror in days.

Asymmetrical was the word I later looked up. I still think about how our lives and bodies are supposed to be balanced. Even when you are strength training, they tell you to pay attention to both sides of the body. When the hairdresser cuts your hair, it's all about the perfect trim. Women with asymmetrical breasts feel self-conscious. If you're working too hard, you're told your work-life balance needs adjusting. You're told to fix it. And that's the thing, I was constantly told to fix my face, to smile better. It's too lopsided, my mother used to say. "Is your face always like this or are you doing it on purpose?" photographers would ask each time I went for a professional passport photo. It made everyone uncomfortable. My smile remains lopsided and every time I haven't had enough sleep, it still demands to be seen in its lopsidedness. Twitching eyes, blinking excessively as I keep trying to see better, trying to remove the fogginess that has become my constant weather. Nothing works and I am out of balance. Guilt arises when I feel I have done wrong to my life and my body. But who to apologise to? I'd spurt, "I'm sorry," to the ones that mattered, and strangers, until it no longer meant anything. They needed to be comforted by the sight of me and I feel as though my body was sinful the way women's bodies are marked as tempting and sinful at the same time. I am tempting to listen to, to look at, but it's not a pretty sight.

As I began to accept that mirrors became another place in which I felt shunned, I stopped looking at them. I still wonder whether mirrors define us, or if we define them. I am still myself, and yet, I see someone who other people would think is lacking. I see the lack before the whole picture, and that is an issue I spoke about at length in all my classes. We want to project the right image for others, the perfect image, and when we fail to satisfy patriarchal or broader societal expectations, we think it's our fault, that we haven't fit the bill. The image of a healthy Middle Eastern girl was no longer what I could aim for and perhaps this has stayed with me throughout the decades after my diagnosis. Mirrors are tools that measure the death of our skin and the dark circles under my eyes became another way to remind me that I was ageing faster than my friends. My eyes constantly looked tired no matter how many hours I slept. I was continuously embarrassed by the number of comments I received about my lack of makeup, my sleepy red eyes, and I began anticipating the comments before anyone ever said anything. The amount of makeup I tried to use to cover my fatigued eyes didn't do me any good. Instead, I looked ghost-like and as washed out as a tie-dyed shirt that had gone bad.

"Young people don't get sick" is the myth I had carried over the years. My aunts and uncles looked at me as though I was a liar. Some didn't hesitate to label me as one. "Girls lie all the time," one aunt had said. "Girls love the attention," another uncle added, jokingly, happily, having cracked the code of women. And that's when I hid at home until I absolutely had to leave the house. I didn't want anyone to see me anymore and hibernated in my room for three dry summer months. My bedroom was a prison to me in its square size, and its blue carpet made it even more difficult to move around. Carpets are not friendly to numbed feet. I have crawled across my room sometimes to reach for a book on the other side of it. Every time I read a book with an image of women who crawl, this is what I remember. Do you remember Charlotte Perkins Gilman's *The Yellow Wallpaper*? And Djuna Barnes's *Nightwood*? Those characters were crawling as they bent their bodies and broke the rules of normalcy. It was an act of subversion. But when it happened to me, I didn't read it as remotely symbolic. I just felt a surge of anger as I recognised carpets were discriminatory.

And they weren't the only objects that seemed out to get me.

Everything around us can be a hazard. I'm reminded of my mother making sure that the house was hazard-free when my baby sister was born. Everything was dangerous. I felt the same way every time I looked at my bedroom door as I attempted to leave the room. I was afraid of wobbling, not just falling. There was a lot more to worry about than just falling. One eye was affected and all I could see was blurriness. Every time I wobbled, the floor began to shake, and as it shook, I knew the floor would win. We have a saying when we are utterly humiliated that means "I wish the ground would split open to just devour me." I had never thought of it the other way around. It was humiliating to be devoured by the floor, something meant just for our feet to wipe themselves on. Dirt. The dirt wasn't the floor anymore, it was me, sprawled across it, relieved and grateful that no one was there to see me.

Every day, bodily maintenance became a hassle. It still is sometimes. We tend to think that these are issues that come with age. I had never considered holding a toothbrush, or the way I cup water in my hands to rinse my mouth, as being difficult before. Gripping a toothbrush, trying to keep the water cupped gently, staring at this new person in the mirror, these are moments that have never left me. I look at my wrinkled face today and wonder what it was like looking at my face then—no wrinkles, yet I still could not take care of basic tasks. Buttoning my shirt was an impossibility. Buttons demanded to be recognised for their grandness. My mother would help me look presentable. Before going to class (as a student and as a professor) I would need her to close me up—a button there, a zipper here, an earring clicked there. Forget high heels, shoes with laces, more objects that would be added to the list of things that suddenly became part of the invisible enemy I was fighting.

As my world began to feel like a war zone, I was constantly trying to fight. What was I fighting? Was it the mind or the body? Was it the mind that had deteriorated, or was it the body that couldn't house my mind? If the brain is located in the central nervous system, then isn't it within the body? What was failing? The randomness of the disease was something I couldn't adjust to. It wasn't cancer—so I wasn't dying. It wasn't diabetes, which was something I had watched my father deal with and didn't stop him from functioning. And I had all my limbs, they hadn't been cut off in an accident. So, what was this random disease, this random disability? As I mentioned previously, I had come up with the term random disability and used it in one of my academic publications. I couldn't understand other disability scholars' surprise when they heard the term. It was a random disability because there were days I didn't fit into the disabled category and other days where I didn't fit into the able-bodied category. This was a body that refused to be disciplined, and yet I felt punished. I was outside of language and knowledge. I couldn't name it, label it, therefore I couldn't conquer it. The ghost of MS continued to live near me, right above my shoulder, the same way we are told we are born with two angels that sit on either side of our bodies, one on each shoulder, recording our good and bad deeds. Except this ghost seemed to linger above my head, zapping away at my brain cells, killing them one at a time. Deaths were taking place within my brain, and I could see some remains on my body whenever I struggled. Only an MRI would give me access to what I couldn't see. And even when a young, handsome, and hip doctor pointed out that I could see the size of the cells shrinking, I couldn't see any of it. All I could hear were words, big words, scientific words. Science was against me, as it had always been. At times, I thought that science was meant to remind us it was the all-knowing and ever-powerful God. But then the handsome Doctor Laith looked at me and shrugged his shoulders, helplessly confirming that there was nothing to be done. You just wait and watch what happens.

o

And so, I have been waiting and watching, recording sentences here and there in my diary, blogging bits and pieces, using social media to vent, and finally, speaking to you, and deciding to share. At times, I will sound as though my experience is the only experience worth listening to, and when that happens, forgive me. I know only what I think I know and what I gather I have felt and what others have shared with me. Our shared experiences and our pain have become part of this narrative. If you can take anything from these narratives, then just consider what it's like to listen, to share, to think about the body and ourselves. We will all become ill one day. It's part of the cycle of life, just like death, but we choose to avoid it, until it becomes a part of us. That is the hardest part. My younger self found it to be a betrayal of the body. I was young and invincible. Today, I accept illness and disability as part of who I am. The way I measure my life in moments of fatigue, energy spikes, and continuous losses, while I gain clarity in other areas. Rumi said the wound is where the light enters, or so my mother says as she quotes him without a real reference. But it was my mother's voice who passed his words along to me. If the wound is where the light enters, then we are all wounded creatures, and if we put all that light together, we are all able to see. I want to see, and I want you to see. So, here are the wounds as they relate to a language pieced together to help make sense of everything we feel, but don't and can't label. Illness is a place of exploration, a paradoxical place of loss and gain. Relationships and human connection are all we keep with us. I think of selves as recycled, washed out, bent, brought forward again to witness life and then to narrate. What has kept me together is the desire to narrate. And it began when I thought I was just like everyone else.

Chapter W of Two

Diary Entry: "My mother keeps telling me that nothing is wrong. Is it denial? Is it a defence mechanism against the inevitable? I don't understand."

"That's a vague and rather short entry. I don't understand either," Yasmeen comments, looking at me for clarity.

What is there to explain when motherhood is a country that I haven't visited myself? I have heard Mama's explanations, read her writings, looked at her art pieces scattered across her desk. It is hard to look away from the darkness that evades her writing and the black paper on which she uses a white marker to punctuate. My connection to motherhood is through my Mama's eyes and her chopped sentences. I possess my Mama in a way that I know I must have done from within her womb. The maternal space is a place of safety and homeliness, and yet everything that happens after we leave the womb is unhomely. I look for Mama in different events, connections, relationships, and question her actions, thoughts, and decisions. She is everywhere, a shadow, a ghost, a being that there is no severing from.

I was my mother's firstborn and her experience with self-alienation began with me. Estranged from her home, her identity, and who she believed herself to be. I was then a part of her body and later to become intertwined with her narration. She allowed me to take up a huge part of her life. Mama bargained to keep me. There are so many stories to tell about her that I will just begin with how she tells it.

o

"You'd keep me on the phone the whole time, the whole time I was working my nine-hour shift. This was back in the eighties and there was no way I could place you in my ear, so I would hold the telephone the entire time, and just let you wail," Mama said.

"Why? Couldn't you just hang up? And what was I crying about, anyway?"

"You couldn't stand being alone. The help I had hired was always around you, but you hated everyone who wasn't me. And you hated me for working. You would cry about how awful of a mother I was for leaving you at home."

"Kids cry about everything. What would I say?"

"You'd say that a real mama wouldn't leave her child all alone, and without brushing her hair. That's when I realised it wasn't only about me, but about what I could provide," Mama continued.

My hair was the first confusion I must have had. Curly hair was not common in my father's family as Bedouin women were known for their silky, long, black hair. My mother's side of the family, Palestinian women, were also known for their white skin and beautiful hair. I was born a bit darker than most Palestinians and with curly, messy hair.

Hair wasn't just hair, it was a marker of good looks, and a good bloodline. Asil. "Asil" is the term used to refer to lineage, where you come from, your origins.

In other words, pedigree. Bloodline is measured through physical demeanour, strength, health, and noble characteristics. Similar to mares, women were at times referred to as "mahra," and the mahra had to be protected, concealed from unwanted pregnancies by a male stallion. They were meant to be owned, loved, and cared for by their men. A mahra would not mingle with just any stallion. My grandfather used to refer to a beautiful woman as a mahra; innocent, chaste, gentle, and of course, with excellent reproductive abilities.

A mahra gone wrong would equate to a woman gone mad, pretending to go mad, broken, feigning brokenness, or simply, ill. In many ways, illness infects the rest of the tribe. Illness in this sense is either physical, mental, or social. An ill mahra is a cause of contamination. To be ill is to be polluted and likely to poison the healthy bloodline. A mahra who runs off with a stallion who isn't considered a pedigree would be rejected from her tribe once she attempts to return. And that's precisely why my grandfather made sure none of his girls married anyone outside of the family and the tribe. When he heard of my illness, he didn't understand what it was. But he did ask me, with a smile on his face, why my mind had gone mad, and what was wrong with my brain? How was my brain broken? He didn't wait for an answer, only shook his head, and walked away, muttering to himself about all the crazy things women do. He covered his face with his ghutra, a signal of shame and of defeat. I hadn't understood then what effect my illness could have on anyone who wasn't living in my body. This sense of individualism isn't available to women or men who come from a tribal background. I don't think it's an issue of patriarchy alone. It's the idea that the collective will always dominate and continue to take hold of everything. A weak link in the collective costs too much. I was that weak link because I was ill.

But before I was ever ill, I was the child of a Palestinian woman who had married a Bedouin man and was trying to negotiate what it meant to be part of this collective identity. She had simply fallen in love with him, with his gentleness, his virtuous character, his continuous giving to others, his providing of help and shelter to those in need. He was a man of his word and a man of words. Poetry flowed from his tongue in everyday speech and continued to be part of his life. He would recite old Arabic poetry and nabati poetry. Oral poetry was a way of survival for the Bedouins and a way of entertainment. It was the form of communication that they excelled at. As my father used to say, it's in the blood.

There is something magical about a man who reads and writes poetry. A man whose voice is gentle, never loud, never threatening. A man who gives you a home and calls himself your backbone. But magic has an expiry date and for every illusion there is an antidote. Sometimes it's too late, and that was what happened when my mother realised she was in too deep, with a marriage ring on her finger and very soon a baby girl who looked at her for breath. When baby girls are born, the world isn't as happy as when a baby boy is born. The tribe celebrates the birth of a boy by killing as many sheep as possible and feeding as many neighbours as the meat permits. A boy is meant to strengthen the tribe and I have always found this strange because of the weight women have to carry. A boy is not an object and does not have original sin attached to him, while a girl does. Being born a girl is an immediate disadvantage as it places you in an unwanted category, another for which there is no redemption. There are many ways to sugarcoat this and there are many ways to deny that for many girls today this is still a very real part of their lives.

But for my mother, gender was nonbinary. I don't mean this in a theoretical sense and I am certain she didn't have the vocabulary to define and label her beliefs. She was a feminist without ever knowing what feminism meant. No first or second or third or even fourth wave of feminism. I am reminded of Gloria Steinem's claim that feminism begins with a little girl saying, "That's not fair!" That very unfairness of the world is what prompted my Mama to push the envelope in her own life, and later on, mine. I try to imagine what it must have been like for her to read Nawal El Saadawi in the late seventies, hiding under covers, afraid that her parents would find her reading the dangerous words. One of her uncles had some trading business in Beirut and Cairo and would bring back some of the latest books by El Saadawi, Ihsan Abdel Quddous, and Naguib Mahfouz. He would urge the girls to read but remind them to hide the books. Most families at the time didn't want their girls reading someone as scandalous as El Saadawi. Her friends would sneak the books to each other during school hours along with other romance novels, which were clearly so different from feminist theory. The novels were part of a romantic series that followed a female protagonist's sexual awakening as she navigated her way through love. Naturally, marriage was the conclusion. And yet she didn't want a typical life, she didn't want that ending, and when she met my father, she knew her life's narrative would turn out differently. Marrying him meant she had to rebel against her immediate family. She was marrying someone of a different nationality and of tribal origins. Her family had never married non-Palestinians. Every girl's destiny was known: marry an educated Palestinian man, someone likely to go to the USA or Canada, someone who would build a home somewhere else. The sense of diaspora that stayed with the Palestinian wherever he went was inevitable. Every home would be up for disappearance. There was an uneasiness about resting anywhere, an anxiety that remained nestled between generations as they passed it down from one to the other, each time seemingly shrinking in size, while the truth was it continued to rest in the corners of their minds. When Mama married Baba, she broke the expected cycle, the predictable plot line.

I have asked her so many times why she didn't expect any dire consequences to her marriage. I asked her whether she had thought of children and lives other than her own. Her response was always a flat, "No!"

"When you're young, you don't really look past yourself. I was twenty-one. There was no one else but me and I loved myself. I wasn't going to deny myself that," she says to me, coffee mug in hand, musing over the past, as I question her. She writes her narrative as she tells it to me, flexing her memory to accommodate my requests. I keep pushing for more because I know she still tries to protect me from even her past self.

Mama struggled after giving birth to me and was shocked by the existence of a real baby when she first saw me. To her, a baby was demanding, clingy, constantly needing a lot more than she felt she could provide. It was a state of confusion, a place between love and hate, a place between exile and home. She felt exiled from within her own body and yet felt her baby was exiled too. There was no refuge and no way she could keep the baby inside of her. There was no way the heartbeats could merge into one. Double heartbeats, double breaths, double the food, and now all of that was gone. A separation that was not a separation but instead, a different creature staring at her, demanding to be fed, bathed, cared for, and loved, even when she felt most unloved, and mostly incapable of love. When she regained her sense of self and her willingness to accept her new role as mother, she began noticing that this was a completely different type of love. This was a love that grew more intensely than the free love during the nine months of pregnancy. This was a love that didn't have an expiry date and would become more terrifying by the day.

As I grew older, Mama began to care about my tears and my pain was reason for her distress. Crying on the phone as she went to work meant she had to find a solution. She would place a small yellow hair accessory in my curls to stop the hair from flowing freely. In her version of the story, this seemed to work. This stopped the hourly crying calls while she was working and as I grew older, we had the hair conversation.

"Curls are unique. Look around you. Why do you want to look the same as everyone else? Curls have a special shape. You can't even predict the shape," Mama always repeated to me.

Even today, I believe in letting hair be the way it wants to be. I hear her voice when I can't tame my curls when my numbed hands can't hold a brush in place, and I'm not sure if I pushed the curl back in place or not. Disease defies order. But I still have my curls, and they defy order, too.

Mama's understanding of my illness continuously shifted as the years went by. Initial diagnosis is always different, a type of initiation story. It is exactly as though you are reborn in a new body and have to

43

grow into it. Mama wasn't sure how to respond to my inability to walk, or brush my hair, or wash it. After a few days of me being stuck in bed, with greasy hair and a distinct odour emanating from my body, she came into my bedroom without knocking and opened the windows.

"It smells like death in here! No more of this fussiness. Get up, you're strong. I know you are stronger than this. You've always been unique, so what if one more thing gets added to the list?" Mama asked, not really waiting for an answer. We didn't look at each other but I kept those words with me, tucked behind my ear, like a pencil I needed every time I wanted to write anything about MS.

Mama had showered me many times as a baby, but as an adult this is extremely distressing. Our bodies are meant to be washed by ourselves, not our mothers. It is a strange paradox in itself, the body that expelled you now cradles you and washes you and you are a baby again. Except that you're not. You're fully grown and you have hairs where you shouldn't have them and Mama needs to help you shave them.

I looked down as Mama took care of the details. Her hands washed my curl-filled head so hard it was like she was washing the MS off my scalp.

"Ouch! I don't wash my hair like that!"

"It's cleaner, you have to get to the roots, and then scrub really hard. What do you have to lose?" she continued.

The first few times Mama took care of the shower it was uncomfortable and I blushed furiously. Afterwards, it became the norm and I just feel slightly shy asking for the bath. I count a few days and then ask so I don't burden her. I've read about people with disabilities being burdensome in old age, and I don't want to be the young disabled one burdening the older woman. I wonder how I will ever be able to care for her in her senior years if I still need her and my clinginess has become a literal dependency.

The first few years of my MS diagnosis, Mama ignored the facts. The neurologist told her to expect the worst and to make peace with loss, that I wouldn't be a normal young woman, I wouldn't have a normal life, and I would need complete care. She looked at him grimly and left, without ever saying a word. Outside his office, where I waited, she let me know that there was nothing I wouldn't be able to do.

"You will go to university. You just can't leave the country. Forget about it. You will stay here, where we can keep an eye on you," Mama ordered.

Mama's decision to keep me near her was never spoken about again. All plans of attending school outside Kuwait vanished. There was no way I would be able to take care of myself when I was still re-learning basic movements.

My first prednisone infusion was spent alone at the hospital. Our family had a driver at the time and he dropped me off as I stumbled across the parking lot to get inside the hospital. There were many members of staff, porters as we refer to them, waiting to escort me on a wheelchair. I refused the help and marched on, careful not to trip. My first infusion was in the emergency room. I lay in my hospital bed with so many other women sprawled on beds next to mine. There was a relentless smell of sanitisers, medications, onion, cheese, coffee, and so much noise. Noise everywhere. I could hear women crying, praying to Allah, shouting at the nurses to call "the doctor."

"The doctor is busy, ma'am, please wait."

45

"I have been waiting for hours! I just need to see him! Call the head nurse!" the woman behind the curtain yelled. I couldn't see her but imagined her to be a big-boned woman unable to accept defeat.

This went on for hours as I dozed off after being poked a few times for a "clear" vein. I listened to music using my CD player, and it was a hassle removing the CD every time it finished and I wanted a change. Those things have a billion steps to them. Each initial step was triple the trouble. There was a quietness within the music. I had stopped enjoying music for its pleasure aspect. Music was just another way of muting my pain and the noise of the strangers begging around me. I felt too young to be in this place and yet all I could think of was when I would brush my hair again and if I would have to cut it shorter to manage. I couldn't keep asking Mama to do it.

About three hours later, I went home. It's funny when you think back to times that seemed excruciating in the moment and yet are eventually muted to just another memory. But memory is so tricky. It was you who were there. You were feeling every second in your brain and in every twitch. When I put this to paper, I don't recall the physical pain, but I do shudder when I think of the loneliness. Emotional pain stays with us and it has been decades since I was that teenager but I can still feel it shifting somewhere between my cells.

The prednisone infusion went on for many weeks and then I had to take a lot of pills to ease the brain inflammation. I also had to watch my food intake. Prednisone activates the hunger centre in the brain. I felt as though I could eat anything in front of me. I was constantly famished. But holding a sandwich with numbed hands is no fun. All the lovely contents would drip out and I would stare at it helplessly. After the first time this happened, Mama was there to cut my sandwich in pieces for me. Mahmoud Darwish has a famous poem in which he states, "Ahin le khobz ommi, w qahwat ommi." Everything that is touched by mothers, good and bad mothers, remains with us.

Chapter O of Two

Diary Entry: "Language has failed me, but worse, I have failed language. I constantly feel misunderstood."

Yasmeen reads the diary entry twice. She pauses and stares at the illegible letters.

"Seems like a paradox, huh?" I ask.

"Yeah, I would think we can't fail at language. But we can't just simply be misunderstood. You've always said that communication is the most important element of any good conversation and any powerful piece of writing."

Conversation. Communication. Clarity and indecipherable words strung together to form a thought, an utterance, and a sentence. My entire world depends on words. My career is one of the written and spoken word. I have used both interchangeably and there were many times where neither method managed to succeed.

o

I grew up speaking two different dialects: Palestinian and Kuwaiti-Bedouin. I also spoke English at home because of the Filipino nanny. Mama taught me that speaking English to Baba was not an option. So, at the early age of five years old, I could differentiate between different words for different people. Not everyone was to be spoken to the same. Tata was to be spoken to in Palestinian dialect and was to be called Tata. My paternal grandmother was to be referred to as Jiddah, never Tata. And that's how I became wary of speaking and being mocked.

After the invasion of Kuwait, my mother's family was not welcomed back to their home. Kuwait had been their home forever, ever since the 1960s, and there they were, exiled. Only Mama was left behind because her husband was Kuwaiti. She was left even more estranged from her family, permanently dislocated. Her personal decision to marry my father was now a political one. Geographical distances were imposed, and no Palestinians were allowed to return to Kuwait. Immediately after the invasion, we attempted to return to our normal, daily lives. But there was no normalcy anywhere.

I recall the darkness of the skies. Mama says it was pitch black all day as well as at night. The burning of the oil wells caused so much pollution that we couldn't tell where the sky began and ended. Everything was broken, but the country was in one piece. We had survived.

And that's when language didn't survive. All the words I had accumulated vanished. Neither Mama nor I were to speak Palestinian in public. Kuwaitis were angry at Palestinians and speaking Palestinian was speaking the language of the betrayer. Kuwaitis felt betrayed by Palestinians, and in order to protect us, Baba asked us to speak only Kuwaiti. Kuwaiti was safer. Slowly, Mama started changing her words, her dialect, her accent. She sounded less like herself and more like Baba. This was the part that made little sense to me. And that's when the language spoken at home had to mirror the language spoken at school and in front of my father's family. Glitches were not an option. Mama didn't want me to be bullied and as much as she tried to protect me from that, I was still susceptible to mixing dialects. At the private American school she enrolled me in, I struggled to speak the proper Kuwaiti dialect. Most of my classmates were Hadar, originating from more liberal families, and my dialect was Kuwaiti-Bedouin, even more of a minority. This was the early 1990s, and most private schools catered only to the select elite. People who came from certain backgrounds and could afford the tuition were the only expected students. I started stuttering around the age of seven when speaking became tied to bullying. Mama suffered the same, except adults weren't bullies. They were racists. Mama and I both didn't belong. We became closer as I grew older.

"And what language did you read in, if you spoke both dialects?" Yasmeen asks.

Mama taught me to read. The first sentence we constructed together was, "I can read." Mama had placed flash cards with words and was teaching me how to construct a sentence in a language that wasn't her own. She didn't want me to fall behind in school, and I was struggling to balance two languages and two dialects. Hybridity was proving to be more about balancing the mixture than fusing it wholly together. There was no whole. Everything could easily fall apart.

That's also when I began to fall in love with language, cling to it, try to find a place in it. Language was a place I could create a new identity for myself, someone I could fashion the way that I wanted. But because I was attending an American school, English became the language that I reverted to. It was a language that could provide me with a sense of distance and

I would remain an outsider to English. It wasn't my first language, it wasn't my native language, it wasn't my mother's language. How could I possibly connect to a language that wasn't my own? I began to think in English and sometimes in Arabic. Love was Arabic to me. Anger was English. Tantrums were thrown in English and I felt that I had a language that wasn't my parents, a tool that would keep them at bay. With time, my haughtiness as a teenager grew with me. It became a little pocketknife that I had tucked in the back pocket of my jeans. I could sharpen it with more reading and use it whenever I felt threatened.

Mama bought me a book every week. We would visit a small bookstore in Salmiya and she would wait for me to choose a book. Pretty soon, I developed an affinity for books with female protagonists. *Little Women*, *Dr. Quinn, Medicine Woman*, anything from *The Baby-Sitters Club*, Judy Blume's books. What I read differed greatly from what Mama grew up reading, and yet she showed an interest in what I was reading and asked me to summarise each book I read verbally. She would ask me to summarise the plot in English and then in Arabic, all the while watching me as I explained how so and so did this and that in endless detail. I think about how there are people who listen because they're natural listeners and others who have to try. Mama had to try. She would deal with her own work, cases that she had to take care of, and yet she would make the time to listen, even if it meant she would stay awake later at night to catch up with her own work. Time was a gift that she always gave freely. As I grew older, I wasn't able to give her as much of my time, and I couldn't return the gift as I began scrambling to succeed in my studies, and later at work, too. We forget how valuable the art of listening is, how irretrievable those moments are. You listening to me today makes me feel the same. How often we long to be listened to, to be understood, and yet we can't seem to find the right words. How many times have you regretted saying something, saying it the wrong way, not saying it gently enough, saying it too soon, saying it too late, or not saying it at all?

Words became the only solace I looked for and understood. The only way I could talk to people was through using a language that could shelter me. I did not feel exiled from English, not until I was doing my graduate work in English literature and felt like an imposter. That was the only time that there was no room for me to take part in the English literary conversation. There was no room for mistakes and any mistake would elicit a dry "well, it's not your native language." Always falling short but somehow not exceeding expectations. You were supposed to make the mistakes because you didn't belong to the language. And yet I felt as though I belonged to the language, but not to British English, not to the accent, because all my teachers had been American. I grew up hearing complaints about how difficult and snobbish the British accent was. They were always better, the Americans, and then the Brits were better when I was at Exeter University for my master's. Everyone was always one step ahead, except you couldn't tell who was taking the lead and when, and I never could learn the steps.

I began losing my faith in language early on in school and remember it started when my speech became slurred and my "s"s became slippery. Words stuck in my throat and I would gasp for air, trying to get them out. And no, this is no poetic metaphor. With time, the words were heavier and my tongue fought to expel them. I wasn't always understood, and I imagined cotton balls remained in my mouth as I tried to feel less ashamed of the sounds that I could and couldn't make.

"Enunciate, enunciate," I keep hearing my drama teacher scream. Two fingers in your mouth, that's how you know you're speaking clearly. Nothing less will do. The fingers invaded the mouth, and the throat gagged, the tongue broke.

And when the tongue broke, I started stuttering when asked a question. My skin boiled and the heat spread across my neck, forcing me to speak louder, speak up, as the professor demanded it. I squirmed in my seat, uncomfortable with the attention. Too many people didn't understand, and I was supposed to be getting better with words. Soon enough, I stopped talking. My grades began to suffer as I couldn't participate in classes. Language was not accessible anymore. Not even English, the homeland I had chosen.

Using my hands to write, rather than speak, was another loss. Tools of the trade began to look terrifying to me. A pencil demanded to be touched, felt, groped. My hand against the pencil, pressing harder, pressing into it, trying to make it do what it's supposed to do. Make my thoughts seen. Let the professor read what I need to say. Pencils disappointed me so I tried pens, and they did the same, splashing all over the exam sheets. Everywhere, a miscarriage. Nothing helped me deliver what I wanted to say, and helpful technology wasn't available at the time. Professors wanted words, and they wanted them now. English majors didn't fail to deliver, but I couldn't carry on. This was a chapter of my life that I have to get to later, it doesn't make sense to jump to it, and if I try to divert away from the breakdown of language, it's because it still breaks my heart.

Language became another vehicle that was supposed to take me places and didn't. I didn't kill language, but I felt as though language was slipping away, constantly betraying me. I had the desire for a strong commitment with language and to be infused with it the way I felt when I read books.

o

Some time ago, a while ago, I wrote about the cartography of the body and the way language fails when it has to exit the body. Let me share it because I can't repeat the feeling, I can't recreate it, and I wouldn't be able to say it better than my younger self did:

> You haven't noticed that my voice cracks as I struggle to get the cotton balls out. Speech is not the interior monologue I construct as a writer. It's the words that sputter out—naked, at your feet. I try to tell you that words fail me as much as I have failed them. They used to be my haven, my home, but the day my tongue got tongue-tied (literally) was the day the doctors told me I should use a marker and a board to speak. It would take time to get my mouth to open again, to stretch and lift and close, to roll words off my tongue as smoothly as everyone else does. Every writer loves their words, but what happens when I can't say them?
>
> And when you saw my library, the books that had saved me, you opened our favourite book, the one with the Arab writer who struggled to fight cancer. She didn't make it, but you tell me that the journey into the self was excruciating and that the body housed her until it exiled her. I think about minds and bodies and mindbodies and whether we talk too much theory and forget about touch.
>
> Months later, I trace your name on my book, the way you wrote it for me. I want to learn the shape

of your writing, the way the letters string themselves together to hold up my name. Holding me up, aligning my spine, and I think about how easy life would be if your pen could take the pain away. To take the pain away is to acknowledge its magnitude, and I don't think I want to tell you about it. If I show you, would you fear the daunting future? Would your eyes cease to pine for me, grasp me? ("Cartographically Speaking: Jisim, Jismain")

I can't deny that I have a huge lexicon buried in my shelves and my mind's archives. But slowly, my mind starts replacing words with other words. An archive of words exists, and I choose the wrong one while I look at the object in front of me. I grab the brush and call it anything but a brush. I look at the chair and forget what it's used for. I ask you to sit where people usually sit, on what?

What is it called again? That word, that word that has a "c" in it—and maybe an "i"? I have tried so many ways to keep track of words and they keep slipping away. It's like trying to hold water in the palm of your hand. It lasts for a nanosecond and then it's gone. An almost.

Letters make sense, still. I have to access them and re-construct words, but today I cannot find any Mama-made colourful flash cards. There are words etched into my literary archive, words coming from everywhere and nowhere specific, no actual origin. What is the origin of the word? Where does it come from? When did I first use it? When did it leave me behind? I think of all the work on semiology and semiotics and how linguistics classes offered so much more than I had ever imagined. Signs and meanings, what a word stands for, what sentences can create discourse, how we imagine discourse in different settings. It's endless. The linguistic descriptions of our nervous system, including the brain, spinal cord, and peripheral system, seem to me too scientific and nuts and bolts rather than poetic.

I feel the letters expand in my heart. The core of me knows what it wants. I feel that all I have is home, Kuwait, my books, and some words, and these words are here, in my diaries, in my sentences constructed half-awake, half-asleep, half-paralysed, half-functional, and they form the skeleton of my memories. I want to quote Kuwaiti poet Fayeq Abdul-Jaleel, whom I read in Arabic, and here I am translating him, in a language so foreign to him and so close to my heart, in a language that would render itself incapacitated by his sword sewn with rhyme. Fayeq says, "I have three things I can't bear to leave nor to replace, and if I leave them, I may lose them forever: Kuwait, a few books, and lots of memories."

Three

Chapter T of Three

Diary Entry: "Home is only my body. But my body doesn't look like mine anymore. I feel rejected."

Yasmeen asks me about rejection and home, and whether I mean exile.

If home is just our understanding of a geographical home, a subjective place of existence, outside time and temporality, then how can my body, and not the other's body, feel like home? Lovers utter "you feel like home" all the time. The word is given so much importance that it forgets there are other ways to belong.

Mama used to say that she didn't belong to places. Places made her feel as though she had to adhere to the customs and traditions of the place. The environment you're in shapes you, she would say. And if you want to be flexible, you can't claim that a person feels like home, nor can you believe that home is a fixed entity. Homelands are taken away, colonised, invaded, signs are removed, car licence plates say Iraq instead of Kuwait, and you wonder whether you made up a home all along. We create spaces to belong and leave parts of us in different people and each home we enter. We so badly want to create a bed that we can sleep in, even if it's our own bed. We leave the watch in the stranger's bedroom and they text us the next day asking if we forgot anything. We place toothbrushes in lovers' homes and try to share toothpaste, all along asking, "Is this home?" I would buy a new toothbrush every time I travelled anywhere and leave it behind, never bothering to carry it back home. But my purple toothbrush would stay with me, always, in my bathroom at my house, hidden beyond anyone's reach, no matter how many strangers would enter my space. Mama would remind me that objects don't hold meaning and that it is us who infuse objects with meaning. I label an object as mine and it becomes mine.

But why are objects so close to our memories and why is it that the smell of hospitals still makes my stomach turn? Why is it that when a lover touches my back, I flinch in paralysing fear? Don't touch my spine. I turned my back to the doctor and when I wasn't looking, he jabbed the injection between my bones. Every time I become feverish, I recall hospital curtains and a small mirror that accentuated the sweat beads on my forehead. I hate small mirrors because they carry so much power and yet they fool you by saying they have none. It's what you see in the mirror that counts, they tell you. Your self-perception.

To heal from objects and spaces we need to find ourselves existing outside of what we feel is home. We become slowly, hesitantly, fearfully familiar with the unfamiliar. How can home become so unhomely? How can my hands reject the beloved pen, the untamed curls, the feel of the purple toothbrush? I feel an urge to blame the objects, but I also feel a deep shame within this body, my home, that is unable to house these objects. My body can no longer dress me, feed me, heal me. Somewhere between my neurons, in the central nervous system, the supposed "powerhouse" of the body, the system has shut down. The lights have gone off—but not completely, they are still flickering, and this is even more unsettling. The myelin sheath is unravelling, and not in the seductive, tantalising way that bodies are unveiled. There is nothing attractive about this process of undoing, nothing spiritually illuminating. I don't know whether my body wants to welcome anything external, the book I want to hold, the coffee mug that needs to be hugged, the lover that needs to be cuddled. It won't welcome any intruders in its space, but it perceives its own parts as attackers, villains it needs to wipe out. I imagine the cells at war with each other, an imagined war, a line of defence so aggressive that it forgets the meaning of truce. A truce is all I want sometimes. Nobody has to win. I just want to still feel at home.

"How can something so familiar become unfamiliar to you?" Yasmeen asks as she walks towards the fridge, grabbing a water bottle that I remembered to refrigerate. People like their water cold, and I still want to be hospitable.

When water loses its taste, you know you're drinking water, and your brain tells you that it's supposed to taste like something you know, tasteless but necessary. Water starts to dribble down your chin and then you don't recognise its wetness against your skin. When someone, a caretaker, a lover, a mother, nudges you politely and then not so politely—to notice and to wipe it away.

o

In one of my classes years ago, I taught the short story "The Sandman" to a group of literature undergraduates who were struggling with the English language. To them, the story didn't make any sense and they couldn't see its intricacies. But a more pressing question was, what was this idea of the unhomely? How can something so connected to us become unheimlich? Struggling to explain Freud's theories, I began discussing our bodies after plastic surgery— because so many of the students had at some point undergone a rhinoplasty. They giggled as I explained how the nose is still my nose but is also black and blue. This doesn't look like my nose, but it's still attached to my body. I can still hear the laughter in the classroom as the students (mainly girls) nodded in unison. One student (I don't remember who) explained that after she gave birth, she couldn't recognise her body as hers, but also struggled to connect with her baby as hers. The baby was real, and no longer housed by her, now an external force that demanded her attention. She could no longer connect to her baby or her body and that just made her feel more ashamed, I suppose. But how can I really tell whether she felt shame or anger? There is no knowing, and all I carry with me is her frustration at not understanding "The Sandman" nor "unheimlich." She had lived her bodily experience and still could not express it.

Bodies tear open, seal back, mend, objects enter and leave us. Life, filth, secretions, death. Everything takes place within this house. I stare at the mirror and can't remember when the bulging beer belly appeared. When did I stop wearing my jeans? When did I stop being able to button my clothes and when did zippers become too complicated? This is some-one else's body, but it is still me in there somewhere. I remember seeing lots of images as I scrolled through the internet, lots of art pieces, photographs of older people looking at themselves in the mirror and seeing their younger selves looking back. It's how we see ourselves as young and invincible that stays with us.

And when you lose touch with who you were, you turn to different techniques, trying to bring back your first home—your first state of being.

They tell you to turn to spirituality, if religion has failed to console you. And it works for a while, but only if you really want it to work. The beauty of hope is that it is a drug that we can take infinitely, and it dies last. There is always more to drink and if you run out, you can turn to different ideologies that you can feed on until you start moving again.

So many beautiful women around me get sick. One after the other. They got sick of holding on to hope. They got sick of the law. They got sick of suffocating in their huge houses, windows closed, doors locked. Houses that shone with brightness and sparkled with the latest furniture from Pottery Barn and high-end stores. Each day, they grew more distant from themselves, a slow self-annihilation. One day at a time. Their bodies weren't their own and at the end of the night he would come in and take what was legally and rightfully his. No questions asked, no flirtation, no foreplay, no play, just duties and responsibilities. As they began to feel less at home in their bodies, they started spiralling downwards into depressive fits.

The body can feel at home within the mind, and the mind can feel exiled from the body. They begin to go quieter. There is a stillness that appears, and then they start medicating. Each drug is prescribed without really talking to them. Private doctors would not have the time to talk—especially general practitioners. A quick five-minute chat would entail a "yes, I would like to try an antidepressant." Many of the women who were in my immediate circle felt that that was the only way out. I don't blame them. I don't claim to understand the human brain, nor do I understand genetic makeup or the way chemical imbalances occur. But I do understand how home can be so alienating and how we can build a fortress within the mind that quickly turns into a darkness that cradles and conquers us. The darkness then becomes a part of who we are, and we can't remember when it first paid us a visit. And when we stop talking, we lose touch with who we are.

Home is not always the place we know how to feel safest in. Safe spaces can be held in classrooms rather than home—and that's what I saw when I started developing close friendships with my students. I became a guide, a mentor, and a place that they could come to for advice and support. As the years went by, I constantly heard the same issues, the same fears, dressed in different garments. However, it was always the feeling of alienation and rejection that they would speak of, in different words, without ever labelling the feeling as rejection. There is an unease about naming rejection as rejection. It's easier to say, "I didn't feel like I belonged." Adding "like" to everything would keep some distance in the air, a gap between the words, between the confession and the confessor. By the time the listener (always me) would allow the words to sink in, there were about four or five "likes" that were summoned to protect the speaker and I didn't really know what we were fighting against. I wanted the words stripped and raw, exposed, out in the air, ready to be mended.

Chapter H of Three

Diary Entry: "I can't believe I still have to go to school if I can't even zip my pants. I keep feeling more humiliated. This doesn't get any better. It's like they all can see me and then are grateful it's not them."

"Wow! What an image! What does that have to do with anything?" Yasmeen asks.

I had lost track of the days since she first visited and was becoming more confused and more dependent on my phone's calendar to remind me of the day. My sleep patterns were worsening, and I looked forward only to our conversations. The more I looked back at my diary entries, the more distant I felt from the person who was jotting down these casual but also conclusive remarks in her diary, almost thinking she was the wisest spokesperson on my life and the grand meaning of it all. Yasmeen had been flipping through the pages randomly because I had taught her that randomness was one pillar of my belief system. The randomness of life, illness, recovery, and the circling back of it all. So, we went back and forth while still attempting to make sense of the themes that Yasmeen had originally wanted to discuss.

o

Having the desire to go to school was an attempt at normalcy, but also a reason to keep surviving. I had a goal. I had originally wanted to go to the American University of Paris for a degree in literature. When the diagnosis came, I was homebound and in direct need of my parents' physical support, and doctors didn't think I could get past a few years without acquiring full disability status. I remember sitting in the neurologist's office and watching a young woman being wheeled out by her father. He was wearing a white dishdasha and had his face covered as though there had been a death in the family. This was a tradition that I had only seen when someone had died or there was something really shameful that the patriarch had to cover his face from—that he felt he had lost face. And by losing face, he would have shamed the entire family. Something about her reminded me of myself. I felt as though I was looking at my future self. We locked eyes for a split second, and I recognised the look of despair in her eyes—I had seen it so many times when I dared to look into the mirror. My neurologist at the time thought it best to stay home, stay safe, attempt to slow down the disease's progression rate and stay away from stress. University life would be stressful and there would be no way around my tragic fate—had I not seen the girl who just left his office, he asks?

I did not think of my undergraduate years as a long procession of days that would add up and finally enable me to obtain a degree. I didn't think that a degree would save me from the impending doom that was approaching. But I did want to keep going to classes, if only to keep myself entertained with stories and poetry. Each professor I met would either inspire me or leave me shattered. This is when I realised that each of us has the choice between behaving kindly and gently with students or being a complete egomaniac. I don't exaggerate here when I think of the many failings of academia. Academia was not accessible to so many students, and at times, I happened to be one of those students.

My freshman years involved difficulties with public speaking classes. My speech still slurred from the remains of a relapse and I was marked with a lisp that was read as "so cute" or "unclear." People reacted differently to my lisp, but the professor found it difficult to understand me and, to demonstrate, stuck one finger in her very open mouth only to say, "Enunciate. Each word should fit between your tongue and the upper roof of your mouth. If you don't do that, I can't understand you." And it was that simple to her. I never could get full marks, no matter how hard I tried to exert myself and work on my posture and body language.

I think about how we always focus on standard assessments and grades, even though the educational system is flawed. We claim that education is for all without considering individual needs, strengths, and weaknesses. Eighteen-year-old me searched for a Disability Services office at the university but couldn't find one. I didn't even think there was a Disability Services office. I didn't consider myself disabled. I just wanted to ask someone what I should do if I couldn't use my hands to write essays in class when professors demanded all of our essays were written in class, using a pencil (not a pen). Have you ever tried writing with shaking hands? When you push the pencil onto paper it stays almost invisible, much too light. A pen spills everywhere or scratches the paper.

I walked into one of the British professor's offices one day to ask him for extra time in writing an exam.

He was calm and gentle, his voice barely audible, the result of old age. He had been teaching at the university for nearly forty years and was nearing retirement, but nobody could ascertain when he would take the plunge.

"What can I do for you? What seems to be the problem?" he asked in the usual academic sense of assuming there has to be a problem.

"Well, uh, I just need some extra time when I'm writing an exam, I have developed a problem with my hands and I can get a medical report to prove it," I said.

"A medical report is unnecessary, no, please, no, no need," he repeated. He was uncomfortable and stared at the wall behind me.

"Right. Thank you, Professor, very much," I replied, waiting to depart his office and unsure if I was supposed to say anything else or simply limp out.

He mumbled something in return and scratched his head, going back to reading without glasses, squinting to see the words in what seemed to be the *Norton Anthology*.

After leaving his office, I had to pay a visit to another professor to explain that I would not be able to make it to classes on time because of having to use the cane. She was light-hearted and had a very bubbly personality. Upon seeing me, her first reaction was a gasp and then she quickly cracked a joke.

"What happened? You must be into sports! There's a reason why girls shouldn't play soccer." She was so certain that it was a sports injury that I nodded my head in agreement. It was easier than attempting to adjust her narrative. This was the story that made sense to her and the vision she had of me. I had never kicked a ball in my life and was too nerdy to even pass PE class without begging the teacher for extra grades.

"Yeah, what can I say? Professor, I just need to tell you, the elevators don't always work, and your class is on the second floor, so it takes me a while to get to class. I don't mean any disrespect and would just love if you excused me," I stammered.

"Yeah sure, sure. You're one of the good ones, no problem," she replied, quickly preoccupying herself with something on her computer.

"Thanks a lot for understanding, I'll do my best to come to class on time," I lied. I knew that she couldn't possibly imagine what it was like to fight my way through the crowds. Each step up the stairs was a war. One step at a time, a lift of my leg, a placement of my foot solidly on the stairs, while others behind me huffed and puffed and swore under their breath. They were always so annoyed with me. Everyone was always late and needing someone to blame. I couldn't say anything except stand back and wait for others to rush past me, while I added precious minutes to my delay.

Another pressing issue was my need for disabled parking. I couldn't bring myself to ask my father to help me with this because I didn't want to embarrass him. He couldn't officially and publicly admit to having disability in his immediate family, let alone it being his daughter. Most governmental paperwork demanded a male figure to get the ball rolling. Women did not enter governmental spaces such as ministries, and if they did, they were likely to be ignored or pushed aside. My father would get most work done in a minute while I would struggle to be heard. But this was something I needed to do on my own. After I arrived at the office that gave car permits on campus, the staff member who was working during the morning shift eyed me carefully. He took the medical documentation from me, which stated my diagnosis clearly, and yet asked me for more information.

"Is this your documentation? Sure?"

"Yes, it is."

"Would you be able to get the same report every six months, in case something changes?" he asked.

"Changes? Like what?" I was baffled.

"Like, if the problem goes away. You'll need to renew this constantly." He shrugged.

I didn't want to admit that the problem would never go away, so I simply agreed to his request. And so, for every six months after that, for four years, I would return to the same office to share my medical report. And it was almost always the same man who would shake his head in disapproval and pray for Allah to heal me. Again, I said nothing in return.

But, of course, I didn't always use my cane even though I had access to the disabled parking, which was closer to the College of Arts Building, where all my classes took place. And that's when the rumours started. That's when I heard snide remarks from my colleagues about how I had used my father's wasta to get me a parking permit, how I had no respect for real disabled people who needed the space. And yet again, I didn't say a word. Sometimes people would approach me to ask me if I couldn't stand the heat, or if I was against doing exercise, or if I wasn't worried about getting fat because I wouldn't walk the long distance to classes? I would just respond with, "I don't know."

What I really meant was, I don't know how you can even ask. I don't know what makes you so comfortable asking me these questions. I don't know how you want answers when you already have a story that seems logical, no matter what it does to me. And so, I developed a reputation for being a privileged girl who was lazy and unable to respect people with "real" disabilities. Slowly, I began to choose to be alone, separated from my colleagues. What I was good at was writing words. And when I felt my hands were failing me, I saw writing as a birthing process. Not as a metaphor, but as a real and tangible process of struggling to get the words on paper. I made many people uncomfortable while I took my time writing. The few friends I had (who were also A students) would finish writing their exams and get up, exit the classroom, looking back at me as they left. They had known me to be as quick as they were—always one of the first few people to finish. There was always a moment of recognition when we got up, a nod of affirmation, or a half-smile that we hoped the professor wouldn't notice. But when the room emptied apart from the professor and myself, I became one of the strangest cases. They wondered what was really happening. One of them asked me if I was playing this game on purpose, if I just didn't want to admit that I was smart and quick. One phrase commonly used was "ward off the evil eye." Sometimes if people were too smart, too beautiful, too perfect, they should be concerned that the evil eye would end their abundant blessings. The too much would become too little. So, in order to guard against the evil eye, one would pretend that the too much was just right, or even under the acceptable state of things. Downplay it. My experience with the evil eye was one or the other—either people thought I was faking it to ward off the evil eye or I was cursed and punished for some unforgivable and grave sin.

Today, every time I watch students write an exam, the memory of shaking hands flashes in front of my eyes and then when one of my students brings me back to the present, wringing her hands out of pain—because long essays are so demanding on their hands—I think about how able-bodied students don't mind calling attention to their bodies, because it's not their bodies that fail them, but an external force, my exam, my demands are hard to meet. Carrying the *Norton Anthology* is too difficult for a couple of them, and when I ask why, I'm met with "because it's just too big" and a shrug of the shoulders.

Zipping my pants was always a task that called attention to my body. I would make sure the slider wasn't open and then double-check again. Sometimes, I would ask my mom to do it before I had to leave for class. Other times, after using the toilet on campus, I would ask one of my friends to do it. It was always uncomfortable for both of us. It also meant that I needed to make sure she was visiting the toilet anyway, regardless of my needs. "Bathroom break" was code for "I need help." She didn't really understand what MS meant but she was happy to help a friend out.

But, like all of us, there comes a day where you tire of asking for help. You get exhausted with tiptoeing around people as you feel your knees start to give out. And then there's nowhere else to be but in bed. The curtains remain drawn and the room starts to smell. You're not sure if the smell is yours or whether it belongs to dust or the dog. The windows stay shut and you won't bother to get up. Until Mama barges in, opening the curtains and forcing the sunlight into your eyes. There's nowhere left to hide except under the wool blankets. Until the dog tries to find you under the covers with her paws and you can smell her breath coming closer. She can hear your mother muttering under her breath about laziness and she urges you to respond to her—even dogs know how the familial hierarchy works. She wants nothing but for you to get up and as much as you adore her for her friendship you envy her for being a dog who doesn't have to pretend to be anything else. We have to keep up the pretence of being alive and well and both states mean the same thing. Alive is synonymous with being well. Mama wouldn't take a half-baked body. She wouldn't settle for anything less than a bachelor's degree. I wasn't allowed to stop going to school. I argued that it was pointless to keep pretending there was any hope if I was turning into a vegetable.

"Stop with the drama. I don't remember raising you this way. This isn't you and you're not allowed to hide from the world. Get up. Remember what Nizar Qabbani says when Beirut is in ashes? Get up from under the ashes like a blooming almond flower in April. That's strength. You get up when there's nothing left of you. Strength isn't getting up when you can," Mama said while patting Flake's back. She asked me to look at Flake for guidance.

"Flake is a dog and can get away with being anything she wants. I hate being human."

"Being human is not that different. She's better than most humans I know. Look at how she gets up even with her weakening knees. She doesn't cower and wags her tail and tries to lift her head up. It's how dogs survive. If predators see you kneeling, they'll attack. She knows how to conceal her pain and only whimpers when there's no one in sight. But she loves you and that's why she keeps fighting her way through. Love keeps her going. You need to feel the love around you too," Mama continued.

"I don't feel love or loved. I don't even like myself," I growled back.

"That's a shame. You shouldn't be ashamed of who you are but you should be ashamed of not loving yourself. Who else is going to do it? Flake and I both will leave you one day and that's the only unconditional love you can expect to have from people. There has to be a place within you that you can borrow from. A reserve of love. It's days like this where you need a crutch to lean on. You need to start building your crutch. Your twenties are the time you either let go or keep going. We all have a crutch but not everyone can tell you what keeps them going. I thought it would be love for you, but I could be wrong. You need to find your own crutch and it can't be something that wobbles so easily!"

Mama left the room after those words and left me thinking about all the possibilities of failure and of giving up. Would it be a total loss if I kept going to my classes? What if I just got that piece of paper and charted it down as done, accomplished? Made Mama happy with it. That would leave me free from guilt— an emotion I couldn't deal with, especially with my mother. She didn't deserve me letting go just yet. If Flake was holding on for me, then surely, I could do the same for my mother?

I got through the rest of the semester and then also the following years. We didn't talk about it again. Anytime I felt the urge to hide in bed, I would remember the look of expectation on my mother's face along with an unwavering belief that I could get up. Whenever my father would see me having to use the cane before going to classes, he would comment using a Bedouin phrase that meant every warrior had to rest before continuing the war. Evidently, the only way he could come to terms with what was happening to me was to understand the disease as a metaphor for war. He hadn't ever heard of illness as anything other than something to be quiet about. It was a war in the middle of the night, an invasion of the tribe, a raiding army that wants to conquer you while you're asleep and defenceless. And if I was at war with illness, then I must be a warrior, regardless of gender. He would say, "This is just āstrāhaT mharib." "Mharib" was a noun reserved for men, but something about my fight with illness made me genderless. This made me triumphant, as though I had risen above being a girl. I was now a warrior in his eyes and all I had ever wanted was his approval. Fathers have this effect on us. We know they continue to have their grip on us even as our bodies transform to womanly bodies, even when we learn the term "patriarchy," and we recognise their behaviour as sexist, we still look at them with a desire both to rebel and to please.

My father needed to see me as a warrior, and I let that myth grow. It became a given—a wobbly warrior who would keep going to school. In retrospect, I didn't think school meant anything more than a place I could escape my bed and the darkness that seized me by the throat every morning.

Chapter R of Three

Diary Entry: "I feel like I understand what resurrection is about. I felt like a human turned into a vampire. Or like Jesus, who had to die only to be resurrected. This is not a myth. I tasted blood in my mouth. I tasted my own beating heart and my cells."

Yasmeen had spent a few weeks rummaging through the diary entries and was now thinking of avoiding the thematic arrangement of the entries. They weren't meant to be categorised so tightly and neatly. Memory is always a liar that fabricates the truth and then claims to tell you nothing but the truth. Any thematic probing will shatter the puzzle. Any attempt at constructing a linear narrative will inevitably make me a liar. I can handle being an occasional liar, I can handle being lied to, but I cannot be held accountable for telling these stories as undebatable facts that hold and are held by myself as the centre. I will not be the authoritarian figure when I can barely tell these stories to her and I am feeling like it is my homework that I need to finish. It is the assignment that the student has given her teacher, and I need to oblige. I had never allowed late submissions. No, wait, that's a white lie. I have. With marks deducted. It was a random allocation of marks that I believed should be deducted. Who was I to say what ten per cent or twenty per cent meant?

Even when I deducted the marks, I would wince at the penalty. And now I felt the same way. I had to provide answers to a question I barely understood. What was the thesis here? What was the whole point of sharing these stories and moments where everything felt fractured? I was getting to the climactic point of this narrative—or the climactic point of my illness narrative, or my life, or the story I'm trying to tell. Like every climax, the tension right before is what propels us to keep going, even when you feel you just can't go on.

"I want to ask if this is yet another metaphor for feeling better after feeling like you're gone? Is this a way out of depression? I've felt really heartbroken before and I remember it felt like I could never love again. But I did. But during the time I was sad, I just couldn't breathe properly. Anxiety pangs kept grabbing me, and I felt like the world was ending. But it didn't end, and that's how I knew sometimes you really have to hit rock bottom to get up. So even when it feels like everything is doomed, you can get back up, even if you crawl your way through. And then I look back and struggle to describe the experience of pain," Yasmeen expounds, urging me to find the words for both of us.

When we speak of pain, we all struggle to find a language to describe its intricacies, agonies, and losses. It doesn't matter how good you are with words. Figurative language is so often used to speak of what pain feels like. Virginia Woolf struggled to find words to speak of pain in her essay "On Being Ill." She claimed we have words for heartbreak and love and so many feelings, but when illness sets in, we can't describe the vast emptiness we find ourselves in. Space becomes empty and even if there is a crowd, we can't recognise anyone around us or even ourselves. This space is not a metaphor. It is the air that we breathe that slowly injects our lungs with a desire to stop breathing. It's like staying underwater, holding your breath for too long, so long that you drown and die. And then nothingness sets in. But this nothingness is where I ended up, and I am not sure how I am still here today. This is a memory that I keep tucked away safely, not knowing just how distant and rusty it has become, thrust deep in the archives of my mind (and body). For me to reach for this memory is to revisit the trauma of death and allow it to resurface without granting it power over me again. Think of every horrifying memory that you want to forget. Every violation of the body. Every transgression against yourself. Most of us don't want to relive it. Once is more than enough. But when we write, when we tell stories to ourselves and others, we are repeating the trauma with a little more distance. As I approach this traumatic memory, I feel the need to hold your hand while I speak, or to look down at my own hands for reassurance that I am still here, in the present moment, safely away from all that is dusted and done with.

And to translate and transcribe bodily pain and emotional suffering I need to acknowledge that I will not give you facts. I need to spin the tale a bit and pay attention to the aches of the heart and the sound of my breath as I recollect the shards that hurt the most. I will use metaphors and allusions and yet I am also referring to a very real and material state of illness and death. My angle of vision is restricted to a kaleidoscope of moments that I can only peer into. The scenes flash before my eyes and I have to look away. But no, I promised you I would stay the course. I have to sit with the discomfort and wait for the pain to dissipate.

o

The doctors were excited. You could sense the anticipation in the air. This was ultimately an experiment of science trying to annihilate nature's course of this disease. The doctors wanted to try to reset my immune system by literally turning it off and back on again, but this time by injecting stem cells into my veins. Stem cells are cells in limbo. They can remake themselves into any cell, depending on the environment they find themselves in. The ultimate chameleons. I won't go into the scientific details and what the hypothesis was. I won't attempt to make sense of it or help you understand it. But what's important to me is to defend myself here. I risked my life by placing my life in the hands of doctors who experimented with human life. This was not an approved experiment, and it was considered dangerous. But for a twenty-something-year-old, the risk is never too high. You believe you are invincible even when they tell you that you are no different from others. You think you're untouchable, even if they tell you death is coming for you. Azrael is just a myth and you smirk at the naivety of those around you. You know better. The cockiness of myself in her twenties is something I look back on and wonder if I could borrow some of it now, if there's a reserve I can reach into and smear myself with the confidence that is much needed now. It's like speeding really fast and then noticing a car accident on your left. You slow down to check out the accident, shake your head at the image of the totalled car and the lifeless body sprawled on the ground. And then you speed again, your mind fooling you into thinking it can't happen to you. We don't think death can happen to us even though we are told it will, eventually.

I stared at the papers and printed my name, not bothering to read everything the documents listed in fine print. I knew fine print was meant to be read, but also wondered who has the time for that? Why the stalling? I wanted an exit plan. A way out of pain. I wanted a working body. I wanted the chance to go to graduate school. I wanted the chance to hold a baby in my arms, knowing I had carried it to full term. I wanted a fuller life, but mainly I wanted a painless life. I had forgotten what life was like without pain. I wanted mornings where I could jump out of bed. I didn't want to fall anymore. I didn't want to live dreadfully anticipating the next blow. The experiment I signed up for demanded a large sum of money—which I was fortunate and privileged enough to receive my mother's support for. My mother took a loan from the bank and continued paying it off. She was willing to pay whatever was required, if only she could buy me more time. We were negotiating with science and asking for an extension on my nerve cells' ability to survive. It was simply a chance to delay the inevitable destruction of my nervous system. This request for an extension cost my mother her entire savings and an additional burden of a loan. What shocks me is how she didn't hesitate. She didn't flinch. She didn't question whether it was "worth it." I begged and cried in her bedroom while she held her Quran between her hands and looked at me, sobbing incoherently. I only wanted a chance, a fighting chance.

"Everyone deserves a chance. And since you have a mother, it's my duty to help you get that chance. You need to access it and if I am a tool to help you unlock this box of hope, I will do everything I can to support you," Mama said, her eyes brimming with tears.

I don't remember how many thank-yous I said. I don't remember how overwhelming it felt to have someone love me this much. Many times, I felt undeserving of all that love, as if I had failed at being human, being a good daughter, and at being worthy of love.

I stood nervously at the underground clinic, waiting to be taken to the operating room. I signed a paper that released the doctors from any responsibility—in case anything went wrong—a word never clearly defined. I was getting ready for a new life, no matter the cost. This is the point where I will narrate the scenes both through the eyes of my older self and my body strapped to the bed.

There's a look of anticipation and hope in my eyes. I nod my head earnestly as the doctor takes my arm and pierces the vein with the long needle. He's done with the left arm and now moves forward to the other side of the bed to grab my right arm. I'm lying with each arm pinned to a huge white machine that will remove all of my dirty, bad blood and cleanse it. Like plasma therapy, but not. I have arms lifted and look like Jesus might have looked nailed to the cross. It's time to begin the voyage into the dark with strength and vigour, summoned from all the desires to be just like everyone my age. Temporary pain is the price for a life free of pain. The doctors ask me about my studies and then about marriage, the two topics that will guarantee a conversation. They need to keep me distracted from the pain, but also focused enough to carry on a conversation.

The male doctor, Doctor Essam, does most of the work. The female doctor, the brains behind the scientific experiment, doesn't touch the patient. But her presence is both reassuring and frightening. She patrols the room and then returns to the bed muttering under her breath incomprehensible words. Doctor Essam looks at Doctor Laila and asks her if he is doing well on time. By then, I am losing control of my ability to stay focused and feign strength. I shudder and the shudders quickly shift to uncontrollable shivers. The chills overpower me and my bones rattle the bed underneath. Am I seizing? Is this what a seizure looks like?

"It's just blood loss. We need to remove almost all of her blood. It's almost over," Doctor Essam reassures my father, whose face has turned a yellowish pale colour. My father nods and steps outside the room, deciding to keep walking away from the scene of my death. My older self follows him outside the hospital to see where he is going. He walks and walks until he finds himself outside the hospital and looks back at the hospital behind him, wondering if he will return to an empty bed and be informed that his child has gone.

Doctor Laila notices her patient is young. Too young to respond well to her experiment. Maybe she should've waited a few more years. But experiments need different variables. Different age groups and various diseases. Each will give her more information and insight into what needs tweaking to achieve the desired outcome: a healthier body that can fight disease with younger cells. But what happens if the stem cells transform into cancerous cells? What if the patient's body can't handle the new cells and starts breaking down? Can she just write these off as failed experiments? That is the whole point of trial and error. Even death is part of the experiment. The idea is to bring the patient close to death. Simply, to stop all their systems right before they truly die and then reset their system with new cells circulating in their bloodstream. The cells will know what to do and they will target whichever organ is deficient. The cells will find themselves in their right home and find a host that they can quickly adapt to. But this patient is the youngest she has met, and she feels obliged to help.

As my eyesight diminishes and my hearing is compromised, my younger self begs the doctors to stop. To just put an end to it all. Over six wool blankets cover my body, but to no avail. My teeth are smacking each other, and my tongue is caught in-between, struggling to say the word "Enough!" There is no magical word that will put an end to the torture, and the doctors know better than to listen to my pleas. My pleading eyes water and there is nothing Doctor Laila can say to make them stop. I lift my eyes to the ceiling where I feel as though the ceiling can save me—something beyond the ceiling, somewhere in the skies, somewhere someone can actually save me. The minutes turn into hours and time will not stop. Begging will not make time speed by, and I can't get used to the piercing needle that is melting into thin skin. Time doesn't heal all wounds, but cements them. I am becoming one with the needles and look like an animal struggling against its slaughterers. Like an Eid sacrifice.

My older self looks at this and can see the tears mixing with blood and vomit. The younger me looks up to the ceiling and then I raise my finger slightly, thinking I am about to die, and want to say, "Ashahadu ana la ilahla ila Allah." I'm ready to go and unafraid. I am begging the doctors, praying for their long lives, please, stop, stop. Finally, I take a deep breath and my lungs wrap around and squeeze my heart, suffocating my younger self. There's no air left in the room and my eyes are bewitched by something in the ceiling again. I can see something more interesting than the doctors probing. I follow the shadow on the ceiling and close my eyes. We both do.

The beam of light was real. The stories weren't just stories. It was a strong light, but stronger in its breeze. The air had left the room, but I desperately needed to breathe and the breeze came to lift me off the bed. Slowly, gently, without disturbing the doctors from their mission. No commotion at all. I was no longer strapped to the needles or the bed and saw myself being pulled up by the lavender gown. Up, up, away. There we go.

I must follow her. My younger self seems to see something no one else does while the doctors are still watching my vital signs. My eyes are closed and I panic as my vital signs drop quickly. Doctor Laila recites the Quranic verses she remembers and reaches for the oxygen mask. I let the doctors try to figure out what's happening to my younger self and instead follow her into the unknown.

My grandma is motioning to me to come closer. Tata's lovely brown curls and rosy cheeks are hard to miss. She looks taller than I remember her. The two of us finally hold hands and I can see that there's whispering between us.

I come closer and I can see that my younger self is smiling and relaxed. She has no idea that the doctors are trying so hard to bring her back. She is happy to be with Tata finally after Tata's struggle with cancer. Now they can both rest and let go of all the darkness that is the world.

And then they begin talking about souls. This world is filled with men and women and divisions by social class and race. But where Tata takes her is beautiful. Everyone is there. Not just people who have passed. Everyone has a soul that is genderless, colourless, free. What is freedom but a place where you float, free from space and time and any barriers? Skin has no place here. Language is unnecessary because everything is said and felt and heard in your gut. Words are the clean air that you breathe, and there is no rejection anywhere. The place holds both Tata and I, and I can see other members of my family and lots of women I don't know but who seem so familiar to me. I can only see shadows—they are not real people. It's like bodies have been compressed to fit into only a shadow. Nothing more and nothing less. But Tata knows who each shadow is and the story it carries.

"Everyone here is at peace, rested and right where they should be. But most have come a long way to get here, like you," she says. "You wanted a better life and ended up here. Come with me, let me show you what love does. It doesn't just heal. Love breaks and beats the life out of you."

Tata points to Danah, the gem, the girl who fell in love at twenty. Danah was beautiful and smart. She had hopes for a bright future ahead of her. She fell in love with another girl and of course there was no room for that nonsense anywhere. And now here's her mother, dead long after Danah killed herself and left behind two little girls. Danah's mother, Nirmeen, was responsible for Danah's marriage to Ahmad, who had no idea his wife was dying a slow death each time he touched her. Danah had never said a word to her mother or her friends or family. She carried her secret to the grave. Her love story remained etched within her cells and never left. But it wasn't a bad marriage. Ahmad was good to her and gave her a big house with pastel-coloured walls and matching couches. He then gave her two golden-haired girls, twins. They both looked at Danah as if she was their whole world and she did the same. But a part of her remained severed with her lost lover. She loved her mother so much that she couldn't break her heart. She couldn't tell her who she really wanted to be with and how she had no way out except if she remained unmarried or left their country. She didn't want to immigrate, didn't want to renounce her religion, and she realised that freedom was not an option for her. Loving her mother and being her only daughter meant sacrificing her lover, the way Ibrahim was asked to sacrifice his son. If Ibrahim had agreed when Allah asked, how could she refuse her own mother?

Nirmeen was the proudest mother on the day Danah wore her silky white wedding dress. Everyone came to the wedding to congratulate her. There is a price to pay for being born a girl and becoming a woman. Simone de Beauvoir said it best: "One is not born, but rather becomes a woman." But what makes you become one is an endless process of stretching yourself thin to fit society's expectations. As you keep stretching yourself and bending over backward you injure your spine. You break your back and can't seem to find who you truly are anymore. Danah kept repeating that she had lost her soul without ever explaining what she meant. Nirmeen held her in her arms as she took her last breath, the mother outliving the daughter. Mothers weren't supposed to bury their babies, but here she was, burying her dead and beautiful daughter. The cancer diagnosis had come too casually, too early, and never made any sense to anyone. But the myth of cancer prevailed. She was too sad. She had lived grieving a part of her soul that eventually she let go. She came here. Danah had crossed over and was waiting for her lover. She wanted another wedding, but this time, a wedding for the both of them.

Tata points to yet another shadow on the wall, this time of a man. Hamad. Here is Hamad, another stranger to me, but yet familiar in his smile. He is fidgeting with his hands and doesn't look up as Tata and my younger self stare at him. Hamad died too early. His body had given up. He was only twenty-nine at the time and had lived his life struggling with alcohol and drugs. But again, it wasn't his fault he had a major addiction problem. Hamad had lived in a well of loneliness, a perpetual state of self-hatred. He wasn't macho enough. He was a romantic poet who couldn't find his place in a society that wanted men to be real men. He was called out for his love for contemporary dance and later on ballet. Hamad was beaten and humiliated by his older brother and two of his male cousins. With time, the rumours spread, and he wasn't able to contain them. The family rejected him, and he found himself unable to associate with them. He didn't feel like he could belong to them or live in the same space. He slowly diverted his attention away from school and family.

Hamad hadn't chosen the degree he wanted to study and was continuously failing in engineering school. He wasn't meant for anything other than English, and yet English was deemed too feminine. He had soft hands meant for pottery, art, and words. He had a gentle soul that craved both men and women. But his body couldn't house him. He felt as though his body was not his and ever since he was very young, he would try to tell his mother that he wanted a fuller chest and more curves like his sister. His mother understood very early on that there was something very wrong with him. She feared for his life. She imagined what his life would be if she supported his confusion. She couldn't let him imagine a different life, so she started telling him stories about what happens to boys who act like girls, how their genitals get cut off, how they get burned by Allah. She hoped that fear would stop him from exploring a different lifestyle. And she was right, because mothers know best. Fear entered his body and slowly grew to suffocate him daily. Hamad's only escape was drinking, and later he began experimenting with drugs. His body collapsed as depression and addiction took hold of him. One day, they found his body in his huge room with his belt around his neck. The family wrote it off as a heart attack, but his siblings and his parents knew it was a last and final suicide. He had finally succeeded. This was the freedom he was looking for all along. Hamad finally owned his life and his body. We are told that your life is not yours and that your body doesn't belong to you. You can't harm it, touch it, kill it.

Tata moves past him and my younger self asks questions I can't decipher. Only Tata's voice is audible. Then I see my father's mother, who had also passed away a while ago. She doesn't notice us walking by. It is like we are ghosts but can see right through everyone's story. She is much younger than I remembered her and is huffing and puffing about something. There is something she is mulling over and it seems to be a book between her palms. She wasn't literate when she was alive. Like all young Bedouin girls, her parents married her off as soon as she started menstruating and she never learned how to write her name. She started giving birth by the time she was twelve years old and kept giving birth for as long as possible. She was a scary woman as she started ageing and was protected by the number of sons she had: twelve, the same age she was when she started giving birth. Twelve boys helped her establish herself as a matriarch. Twelve boys were a whole tribe. That was enough to sustain her until she started ageing. As she became weaker and frailer, she lost her sense of solidarity with her boys, who were now men. Each had moved on to start his own family and to another woman's arms. Her own husband had neglected her and being older and sicker left her undesirable. She accepted that fate, that no matter how much she loved them, they couldn't love her back the same when she lost her health. Love was reserved for stronger and younger women who could bear children and raise them. An old woman with a grey moustache had no place in the tribe. So, she started sleeping alone in a room with red couches and stopped seeing any meaning to daylight and night. She passed away quietly, with no one noticing, and with no commotion.

There are many others stacked like shelves of shadows, traces of people left behind, roaming freely, light as a beautiful breeze in broad daylight. There is nothing disturbing about their presence and the air tastes like cotton candy in my mouth. And that's when Tata looks at me and spots me looking at her and my younger self. She smiles knowingly and tries to push my younger self back outside the tunnel.

"You'll have to go back the way you came. But it will be dark as you head outside. Close your eyes really hard. Shut them like there's soap in them. Like you're having a nightmare. And then open them as quickly as you can. Put all your strength in the opening. Use your eye muscles and lift your eyelids up. You'll be back in no time," Tata urges.

My younger self must resist her request because she shakes her head adamantly.

"My daughter is waiting for you. Mama loves you and needs you. And you are never ever alone. You just think you are alone but there's more to everything around you than you can see. We live around you; you just need to feel the breeze. Just listen to the sound of water as it touches your skin. Follow the breeze that lifts the leaf."

Meanwhile, as my younger self listens to Tata and begins walking through a long alley that looks deserted, the doctors increase the oxygen delivery. Vital body signs show my body is no longer functioning. But a breath finally enters my body and I receive it, I inhale it, and suddenly, with a sigh, my vital signs return to normal. I look like I have soap in my eyes and struggle to open them.

Two pairs of eyes open at the same time. I am one with my younger self again.

The doctors are more excited than relieved. They look at me as though a miracle has just taken place. Doctor Laila falls on the floor in prayer position and thanks Allah for this miracle. She then gets up and starts speaking words of encouragement at me. She is proud, she is happy, she knew I could do it.

"We did it together," Doctor Essam interjects.

"Of course, of course! Now she's a real baby. Reborn! Allah always wins!" she proclaims, wiping my messy hair away from my sweaty forehead.

Chapter E of Three

Diary Entry: "Sometimes falling in love with the mirror image of you fails. Sometimes men have it easier than women. But sometimes they don't. I can't tell which body is worse."

Yasmeen considers the journal entry in front of her and then takes a sip of the lemonade I had made for today's visit. We are still meeting at our usual hour, half past noon, and have organised most of my book-shelves. She has grabbed a few of my critical theory books and the duplicate copies of Arundhati Roy and Jeanette Winterson I have lying around. I shrug my shoulders every time she picks a book and feel as though they no longer belong to me. I used to be very protective of my books, of moving them, of lending them to others. Each book carries a memory and a time that becomes embedded in its spine. But now that my spine is filled with lesions, I feel the books need to be freed from my possessive hold. My obses-sion with things is easing and I can let them breathe, as I learn how to breathe by releasing. I release my grip on my things, my people, my memories, and my desire for freezing time.

o

When I finally joined the MS society, I met a man of around fifty years old, sweet, gentle, and almost always struggling to speak. He spoke to me when no one else would at the first meeting that I attended. Sometimes the universe places someone in your path who will speak to you when you need it the most. That someone for me was Ghalib. Ghalib, whose name means "winner," was not a winner by any usual sense of the word. MS defeated him. His words never could make sense and I learned to strain my ears when listening but also to read his lips. His words were barely audible, like a whisper, and he wore a white dishdasha at all times, without a ghutra. He belonged to the richest family in the country. His privilege was clear: he would arrive with two Indian helpers, a man and a woman, one who was a driver, and the other who was a professional nurse, always there to assist him. But I never saw his family join him at these meetings. Ghalib was very attractive to me at first. His presence demanded attention and respect, even when he struggled to speak. His voice was barely audible, his vocal cords affected by MS.

The group at the MS society comprised around twenty people—I could be wrong. The numbers are no longer clear to me. People would come and go. There was nothing consistent about these meetings, and many people who attended would not come back. Some were full-time members, attending every meeting, active in every event that took place, and frequent public speakers. I must have been the youngest person there at the time, which further isolated me. I was embarrassed by my ability to walk while they were limping or using mobility aids. I felt ashamed to claim the same disability status. How could I walk among them and feel innocent under their stares? In retrospect, I am certain that it was my anxiety that accentuated the feeling of encroaching upon their personal space. I saw myself through their eyes and found an imposter, a drama queen, a liar. There had to be a space for people like me, people who weren't familiar with real suffering. I was too privileged and I could see the women staring at me. The men avoided looking at me because I was so young and my blood was too fresh; it was culturally inappropriate. I tried to hide myself with my long black hair and let it fall in my face. As the years passed, I withdrew deeper into my body, although I felt so alienated from it. I barely could recognise it anymore. After the stem cells procedure, I had gained weight and had difficulty moving because of the added weight. The weight gain resulted from the shift in my estrogen levels. My hormones were all over the place and I struggled to maintain a feminine look as testosterone invaded my cells. There was an imbalance of hormones because of the stem cells in my body. I realised more and more how hard it was to maintain an ideal female silhouette. Under the male gaze, I felt like a fraud. Under the female gaze, I felt a deep sense of shame. Everyone seemed to come with their own baggage, shifting their weight to get to the middle of the room, a circle with a small plastic white table in the middle of it. On the table was a jug of Arabic coffee and tiny red plastic cups. As each person asked for a sip of the coffee, the helper brought forward their cups and then looked at me, standing at the edge of the circle. That's when I realised I had to move forward and join them.

Ghalib was seated next to the men and noticed me. His look wasn't intrusive and I locked eyes with him and was curious about his story. The silver moustache and beard highlighted his dark eyes and his upper body leaned forward as if anticipating the newcomer. The leader of the group, Amna, ushered me over with a wave of her hand. Her fingers were covered with expensive rings and I wondered how she could afford to wear them; how difficult it must be to put them on and then remove them. Then I noticed the excessive use of makeup. Her eyelashes stood out, as if protecting her eyes, her colourful hijab stood in sharp contrast to her black fringe, which I could see was peeking out. I was unable to wear makeup for the longest time unless someone was helping me. It took too much precision, focus, and steady hands that stood the test of time. No shaking allowed. I thought again of how difficult it was to create the ideal feminine look. Women always have to look so perfect, always waiting for the right suitor to come find them. It's like chemical signals of availability. But I had also read so many so-called scientific studies that mention how we are only attracted to healthy and symmetrical bodies. A lopsided smile would be asymmetrical so how could anyone actually look my way? Lipstick would highlight my droopy smile. I had faced too many unsolicited comments about my smile and its sloppiness. One of my close friends had asked me if it was a seductive tactic, a way to appear more feminine and flirtatious. And whenever I had to take actual professional photographs I would tense up and feel the anxiety kick in. Every photographer would pause and inquire about whether I was doing it on purpose.

But I shook off all the comments and started to think that smiles weren't that important. I sometimes avoided smiling altogether. It was just easier and I learned to chuckle softly instead, while looking down, to avoid locking eyes with whoever was listening. But when I started speaking to Ghalib, I began to remember how intimate eye contact felt. Eye contact from anyone was something I had missed and I was able to slowly bring it back to my life through my friendship with Ghalib. He was the first person to ask me why I was hiding from the group, and whether I didn't want to be here.

"I do, of course I do!" I replied, embarrassed.

He smiled softly and adjusted his square-rimmed eyeglasses. He highlighted that none of us wanted to be here. This wasn't a place you go to for pleasure, like the mall, like a coffee shop.

"You come here for survival," he said.

But to survive, we need to look at the trauma. We need to know that we have fallen down and start looking for ways to get back up, or at least get ourselves to the nearest shore. And in order for me to look at the trauma, I had to first look into the faces of those who were also fighting the same battle. I wanted to pretend I was alone for the longest time and wear a badge of heroism in silence. There was a lot at stake when confronted with having to speak. I never wanted to speak, and I believed that my silence was a silent revolution. But when I sat next to people who looked different but were here for the same reason, I realised I wasn't that special. There was nothing unique about my fight.

I listened carefully to the men as they spoke loudly and watched as the women laughed heartedly. Everyone knew everyone in the group and then they all looked at me expectantly.

"I don't have anything to say, thank you for allowing me to be here. I have MS and I want to get a PhD one day," I stammered.

"A PhD in the mind and nerves?" a bulky-looking man asked. He leaned forward looking for the answer.

"No, just in English," I replied.

"English needs a PhD?" He frowned.

I nodded and smiled, unsure about the sentiment behind the question. I didn't expect him to understand. I didn't expect anyone to understand. I had grown so used to being ignored that it didn't faze me.

The rest of the group began to speak about their experiences with their symptoms and quitting their jobs because working had become nearly impossible with the rapid decline of their bodies. The men started patting each other on the back whenever someone said that he was a happily retired man. Next to me, a woman with shoulder-length black hair shifted uncomfortably in her seat. She had lots of acne on her skin which I noticed was not hidden even with the makeup. I also noticed that like me, she was uncomfortable in the group. I wanted to speak to her but I was too shy and instead just waited for her to say something in this talking circle. She didn't say anything except to the older woman sitting next to her. I overheard her saying that the divorce papers were being finalised and that she was thankful Allah had helped her throughout the whole ordeal. There was more to her story that I hadn't caught but I was surprised that she was mentioning divorce as an everyday occurrence. There were words that were too heavy, too culturally burdened, and I wasn't used to women saying them. I almost wanted to ask her if she was sure about her decision but then reminded myself that newcomers are not meant to be so nosey. What was it to me if some woman had chosen to get divorced? Had she really chosen the marriage? What if she was the one being rejected? It was bad enough that most of us weren't getting married and to hear that divorce was a possibility too made me even more terrified of the prospect of human connection.

When it was Ghalib's turn, he spoke softly and

quietly. The entire room seemed to mirror his calmness. He began speaking about the importance of getting more doctors to speak to families and not just patients. Family is supposed to be involved, he insisted. Families are part of the problem and part of the journey.

"Look around you," he continued, "how many family members are actually here? Most of us are with the helpers we hired to care for us."

Although his comment was uncomfortable and sliced through the air between us, he and I locked eyes for a while and I nodded at him in recognition of his words. Afterwards, he asked me why my parents weren't with me, or if I was married, where was my husband? His questions didn't feel invasive. I don't think anything Ghalib said would have been upsetting. He was the only one who seemed to have a knack for speaking the truth and not offending you. I began telling him about my family and how I had to sneak into the meeting because I didn't want them to disapprove. They didn't want to believe I was sick.

He nodded and listened empathetically and then started explaining that it was the same with his wife and children. They had left him to the care of his driver and helper, and he was learning to cope with that. He also had a dog and a cat, and he started drawing comparisons between people who leave us and animals who become our companions. There was nothing to say except to agree with him, even though I hadn't been abandoned yet, and I hadn't tasted the bitterness of love and heartbreak.

"But the secret is to show up. To the meetings. But also, to everything else. We need to show up for others in the same boat, but also for ourselves. I am proud of you for taking the step towards this place and I'm sure it was so scary. But I think you're tough, just like my eldest daughter. Girls really deal with pain differently. They use all their anger to lift themselves up. And we think women are created from Adam's rib. I don't think Adam would've learned anything about strength if it weren't for Eve—who supposedly was born from his weaker rib. Only those who know weakness, who are weakness, are actually the bearers of the secrets of the universe. Allah places the secrets and the light in those who limp, stutter, and are bent over backward while the rest stand up," Ghalib said, finishing his speech while looking behind my shoulder at another young man who was approaching us with his cane in his left arm.

That's when I met Dhari. He was tall, skinny, and had really thick eyebrows that stood out against his pale skin. He was another one of us, and he was exactly my age. His eyes lit up when he noticed me, and butterflies fluttered in my stomach. Something about him was magnetic, and the way he moved was confident and light—something I had long forgotten. Ghalib shook hands with him and introduced us to each other. He highlighted that we looked around the same age and then asked us when our MS birthdays were. We both were diagnosed at the same time, same year, and we were both nervous looking at each other while Ghalib was extremely comfortable in our presence.

When Ghalib motioned for his helper to wheel him out of our way, I was left with Dhari while the others started leaving the meeting room and then the building. We talked for a little under an hour and I remember having to leave because of my curfew. I left him standing near the main gate of the building, and I believe that's the moment he decided there was something worth pursuing. It didn't take him too long either. Within a few days he had looked me up on Facebook and started chatting about the importance of having a partner who understands where your body is at and where it could end up in a few years. But what was more important, he said, was a partner that didn't judge you for the illness. Able-bodied people always would. People who had different bodies (the way we used to have good bodies) could not get too close to diseased bodies.

"And that's why I want to get to know you a little bit before speaking to your parents about a marriage. I do feel I am looking for the right person to share my life with and I don't want a traditional marriage. I feel like I know you already. I know what the pain is like. And that, to me, is enough knowing. That's as deep as it gets. Skin-deep," he said to me.

I asked him to give me some time to think. I didn't think, though. I pushed him further away from my thoughts. I didn't see myself able to carry a child. It was hard enough trudging along when it was just me. An added weight onto my quivering legs wasn't an option. Growing older without children filled me with cold dread. There were no other women around me who didn't have children. None who remained single. It wasn't a place for single women to thrive, and I was afraid of disappointing myself and my parents. And Dhari was a great man, as my definition of greatness had been at the time. All I saw was a fighter. Someone who would get up every day and fight the same fight.

The courting period continued for a few weeks and then he ended up in the hospital. He had a relapse and was unable to walk or to sit up without tremors coursing through his torso. He refused to see me when I asked to come visit him at the hospital. I kept wanting to visit him and drop off some books to keep him company and Ghalib told me to keep asking him for a chance to be around him. Ghalib explained that sometimes people want to hide but we need to join them in their hiding place until they're ready to join us outside.

Dhari finally agreed to my visit. I carefully chose books about positivity, self-help, religion, and an alternative reality. I didn't own any of these books myself, so I stole them from my mother's library and hid them in a big green bag and marched myself to his room at the Neurology ward. I made sure none of his family members were there before entering the room.

His faced beamed with happiness. He lit up with joy and quickly tried to get up to greet me, arms open wide. He was like a little boy running up to meet his mother after his first day of school. Except a little healthy boy can fling himself into his mother's arms. Dhari fell. He simply fell and hurt his jaw and I found myself on the floor too, helping him back up. His weight was a lot for me to bear, and I felt my knees shake as I tried to muster all my strength to push him off me and back onto his bed. His long skinny arm was around my back and shoulders, and at that moment I realised this was the most physical contact we had ever had.

His eyes watered and his face boiled with humiliation as he reached for the bed's crisp white covers, almost as if he was covering his fall and bandaging his bruised ego. He frowned at me and asked me how I was feeling, trying hard to ignore the elephant in the room. I sat on a white plastic chair next to his bed, unsure of how stable the chair was. I had fallen into the rabbit hole and I was in a strange and unfamiliar place with unfamiliar creatures. This was the hospital room I was too familiar with, the room I knew too well. Here was the uncanny smell of disinfectants that flared your nostrils. But it wasn't me sprawled on the hospital bed. It wasn't me who was embarrassed, and yet I could feel his humiliation spill onto my skin. I repeated prayers and words I had heard others say to me. I felt as though I was a performer, an excellent liar. Things would not get better. There was no telling if he would get better. And yet there I was trying to convince him that this, too, would pass. I told him it was only temporary pain, just momentary, knowing fully well that his body was under sustained attack. And who was to say that I wouldn't be following the same path?

I know that I left Dhari as overwhelmed as I was. When I said goodbye, his eyes were staring at the wall behind me and he nodded quickly, before I could finish my goodbye speech. I wanted to run away from him and the awkwardness in the room. I wanted to go back to my life and pretend he never happened. But when I got into my car, I received a text message from him: *You're the one I will marry.* As I set my mobile down, my hand shook frantically and I couldn't tell if it was a tremor or just nerves, the right kind of nerves. His persistence had been unfaltering but this particular message remained etched into my mind. I had always wanted a proposal to be a question, a request, a coaxing process.

When I went home that day, I sat my mother down and informed her of my decision to marry him. She listened carefully and peered at me from above her glasses. She scratched her head as I went into a long monologue of why I should marry him.

"But he's sick. He can't take care of you," Mama interrupted.

"Mama, I am too. Can't you see it? It's perfect. We both will take care of each other," I replied, flabbergasted with her response.

"You mean neither of you will be able to take care of the other. And what happens when you have children? They'll end up taking care of you. Why would you do that? Why can't you just be satisfied with your lot in life? Live alone. Figure it out as you go along. There's no need to further complicate your life."

There was no convincing Mama. I told her I didn't want to reject Dhari. What if karma came looking for me? What if breaking his heart meant someone else would break mine one day, calling me too disabled? I knew little about karma and I didn't know how the universe worked, but I knew that rejecting him would entail punishment from the grand forces swirling in the cosmos. I already felt like a sinner. I didn't want to unleash more wrath from the world.

"You're marrying him like a martyr would. This isn't love," Mama replied.

It was the first time I had paused to listen to how Mama defined love. All along, I had believed that love was about sacrifice. It was about martyrdom. A good lover was a good soldier, a good nurse, a good caretaker, and there were no limits to what constituted bending over backward. If you could bend, then you ought to bend until you break. Wasn't this what love was all about? I shuddered to think that I had been wrong all along.

Mama and I spoke at length and I listened as tears streamed down my face. I was trying to be a good girl. She kept shaking her head and I had never seen my mother so adamant about saying no consistently to all my suggestions. Sometimes one conversation sticks with you like a birthing memory. All my notions of

gender and disability crystallised. I had been inter-
nalising society's expectations of me as a woman and
I felt like a failure. My only redemption was through
marrying a man, but someone who was also disabled.
I wanted him to accept me and take me in. I wanted
the world to bless this union and here I was not receiving my mother's.

It was Ghalib who told me the best way to deal
with Mama's refusal was to ask her to simply listen to
what Dhari had to say, or for that matter, any woman
from his side of the family who would speak to my
mother. She listened when I told her about my older
and wiser friend Ghalib who was negotiating on my
behalf. Mama agreed to listen. When Dhari's older
sister called my mother to express her brother's
desire for marriage, my mother asked her about his
health status. The sister refused to divulge any information and kept repeating that he was a man, a man
who would always be flawless, no matter what. A man
who would carry any possible shame with him and not
spread it like women. What was the problem, then? My
mother then told her that she was concerned about
our future together as a disabled couple.

"I don't understand. How are they a disabled couple
just because Dhari is unwell?" I heard the question
clearly because Mama was using the loud speaker.

"My daughter is unwell too. That makes two," Mama
enunciated slowly. She gestured to me to come closer
to her. It was like she was showing me to the stranger
on the phone. Would his sister place a higher bid?

"I didn't know she was sick. Dhari never said
anything about that. I see. Let Allah decide then," she
said solemnly.

And with her ma'a al-salamah, she was done, leaving us with no peace. The conversation ended there,

107

but Mama and I sat on the couch next to each other, silently speaking to each other's thoughts.

"Maybe he was going to tell her," I said, without looking at my mother.

"Maybe he couldn't. He was too afraid of her reaction because he knew what it would be."

I had little to say after that because I couldn't defend Dhari and I was tired of having to defend my case. Mama was right, and that was that. I just hadn't thought of the possibilities of rejection that wasn't initiated by me. That night, before going to bed, I sent Dhari a message with a firm no. I wanted to feel as though I had some control over the situation and to salvage whatever was left of me. He responded with profuse apologies but did not call me. His hesitancy further confirmed my doubts and anger. I couldn't understand how he was any better than me.

When I told Ghalib what had happened, he paused for a long time. He listened to my rant and my frustrations over coffee at a café which was the most accessible we had come across. The wheelchair ramp was part of the café's building and, before my illness, I had never noticed or thought about it. My struggle was lifting a cane off the floor and plopping it onto the staircase. Ghalib was comfortable navigating the world in his wheelchair but was extremely angry about places that he couldn't visit because of lack of access. He had tried writing up countless proposals to different ministries and was still waiting on action. I learned the word activist from him. He would repeat, "Everything is a problem we have to solve. If not us, then who will?"

I was young and didn't think of anyone outside myself. I thought problems were creations of our minds and not a physical reality. I had stayed hidden for too long to understand that sometimes our social realities are part of the problem, if not the actual problem. The social obstacles were part of the experience of disability. Buildings and architectural spaces were just extensions of the people that denied us access to fulfilling lives. I paid attention to the details around me and saw the world through his eyes. Because he was older, I listened with both curiosity and trust. Ghalib and I were intellectual friends who shared books, poetry, and analysed how other people dealt with their pain. He would urge me to think about the language of pain. All people spoke of pain. It was just about understanding the dialect, the accent used, reading their actions and reactions. He insisted that our experiences with illness were not too different from other oppressions like social class and race. He used no terminology, but instead, he pointed to actual people we both knew. He pointed out that my experience with disability and being rejected by Dhari's family was typical and not too uncommon. Women with disabilities hurt more because they have to reconcile with their own body and how other people accept or reject it. They must contend with both sexism and ableism. But I was privileged enough to have access to medicine, university, and basic needs. I hadn't been forced out of school like Noor. He urged me to think about how Noor and I were different.

I didn't know Noor at the time, but when I came to know her, I noticed that not all women were the same, and not all disabled women had the same experiences. This might seem like a given to you, but for me it was a moment of growth. I decided to reach out to Noor and befriend her. She loved stories even though she wasn't allowed to pursue higher education. Her dream was to study Arabic literature and her crushing fatigue had stopped her. But it wasn't just the fatigue and MS, it was her parents who believed that her illness would continue to be exacerbated if she attended classes in the scorching heat. Ghalib had been her confidant for a while before her husband put an end to that friendship. She had recently gotten married to an able-bodied man who had stopped her from being friends with any other man.

The worst part was that she hadn't informed him of her illness. She had to fake her status as a healthy, young, energetic woman. Her family had disapproved of her desire to be honest with him. It was too risky for her to tell the truth about her body's mishaps. But like everything that is hidden, it had to come to light at some point. He was sharing her bed and didn't know she was taking any medication until he saw the injections hiding in the tiny refrigerator, the little piece of private necessity that she had requested would be hers alone. When he brought the injections to the kitchen and threw them on the kitchen table, the box opened and a bunch of the injections fell to the ground, landing next to her feet. She was speechless and her ability to hear him began to muffle. Ever since, she had lost her hearing in one ear and nothing had changed except now she was divorced and with the memory of his attack ringing in her deaf ear. Noor was now struggling emotionally and was staying at her parents' house until the divorce papers were finalised. Ghalib suggested that I reach out to her and let her know that I would be happy to go out with her for some shopping (girls' stuff, he had said) or just a cup of coffee.

"Everyone needs a friend. You can't ever have too many of those. Women need to stick together and disabled women need to have each other. I would love to be there for her but she has been too ashamed to return my calls. She feels like she abandoned our friendship but I feel sorry for her. She can't see the bigger picture. She did the right thing by letting me go—even if her marriage has failed. Her parents might allow her a chance to rebuild her life after the marriage. Who knows?" Ghalib mused, and added, "you'll find out soon enough."

Perhaps because of my complete trust in Ghalib, I did as I was told and allowed him to guide me through the awkwardness of getting to know people like me. I had stopped making friends ever since the diagnosis, and I was struggling to make friends outside of school. It was so much easier making friends when younger. This felt strange, and I needed Ghalib cheering me on.

Noor was more than eager to get to know me. She was excited and thanked me for reaching out to her. When we sat down together for iced coffee (we couldn't drink anything hot that could increase our bodies' temperatures) she couldn't stop talking. She was thirsty for conversation and needed to ask a stranger whether she was in the wrong or right. In other words, was her husband a monster for divorcing her, or was she the monster who betrayed his trust?

Like most women my age, I went on a long rant about how all "men are mean" and there was nothing anybody could say after that. This was a mere fact of life and to challenge that meant you weren't mature enough to see the harsh reality, the battle of the sexes. I couldn't think otherwise and was raging with Noor's description of the long divorce ordeal. She had lost so much: her life before the marriage, her life after the divorce was now shattered, and she didn't know where to start picking up the pieces. She felt as though she should start studying. She had failed at maintaining a successful marriage and was thinking of convincing her parents to give her a chance with school.

"Or maybe they don't need to know. But wait—then I'll be lying to them. Am I always going to be a liar, just to get the things I need?"

I paused to answer her but also shook my head. It was a definite no. She wasn't a liar. I still think about Noor's question and now have a different answer to it.

She wasn't a liar, she was a chameleon, and not by choice. It was a matter of survival. It was a matter of balancing her desires with the world's desires. The world wasn't giving her a fairytale ending. She had wanted the husband, the beautiful white dress, the happy and healthy babies. What was so wrong with that? Who didn't, at one point or another, want all of these boxes ticked? She fell asleep and allowed the dream to take her into his arms but then woke up with a jolt that deafened her senses.

But what I did tell her at the time was to go back to school. There was one university that catered to work- ing students, people who had jobs in the morning, and people who couldn't afford traditional learning. She eventually enrolled in the school and disappeared into her books. She stopped calling and asking for coffee, which I took as a sign she had found her path outside the darkness.

For many women living with disability, I found that there were three different life paths. The first was if you were able-bodied and married and suddenly got sick. The husband would likely choose to remarry as polygamy would be the option available to him and most women consented. Islam had allowed polyg- amy with certain reasons, and this was a good enough reason: wife failure due to unforeseen circumstances. The second option was Noor's case, the big D-word.

Divorce, to be divorced, be done with, be discarded after a failure in her ability to pass as healthy. The last option was mine: irrevocably separated from able-bodied men and disabled men. I had never felt that being a woman was as heavy a burden until I felt the scarlet letter of disability wrapped around my neck. The heaviness weighed me down and continued to push me away from people around me. It pushed me so far away that I ran to academia. I wanted to run faster and faster to avoid falling like Noor, like Dhari, like anyone else who had loved and lost. I knew I loved stories and books, and I wanted to try to see if I could establish a lifelong relationship with academia. Maybe embracing a fictional world would help me under-stand the real world. Maybe being called "Professor" would help me be seen. I was tired of being unseen and exhausted of hiding.

Chapter E(II) of Three

Diary Entry: "It doesn't matter if I get to the finish line or not. What really matters to me is that I am trying. At least I got to see the outside world. I'm grateful I'm still here. But I can't decide whether I'm becoming slower and less smart or I'm just losing hope. I'm counting down the days until I get to go home. I am a stranger in this land of whiteness. But I think all I need is literature to get me through."

How do we move forward in the narrative? How does it get better? Does the universe owe us an explanation? For me, none of that happened, but I have had my journey, albeit always interrupted, always on the edge of being, becoming more or less than expected. I remember first arriving in the United Kingdom and noticing the green. Green everywhere. As I looked onto the path that led up to the school I was attending, I noticed that the path kept moving upwards. It was a hill, and then another hill, and the incline would get worse. I paused for a long time and couldn't understand how the actual environment was structured in a way that wheelchairs wouldn't be welcome, that limping bodies and canes would struggle to rise against the ground's pushback. This wasn't architecture. It was just England's nature.

"But did you think you could make it, physically? That journal entry sounds like despair visited and lingered," Yasmeen interrupts.

As much as I wanted to be seen, I still wanted to remain hovering in the shadows. There, but not fully there. Seen, but not fully. Before graduate school, despair came and took parts of me. But I was already rebuilding myself and gathering the fragments to create another life, another self. I wanted more than anything to allow myself to attempt that path—that path that didn't look like it was mine. Academia looked difficult and had no place for people like me. It said so in the university regulations. If I wanted a scholarship, I would have to be fit and free from "issues." There was a medical report that had to accompany your application. I wasn't able to do that, and for the first time, I felt rejected by a larger entity than a man. The culture of academia presumes those best suited for academia are people who are able-bodied and can demonstrate discipline and productivity. There is no place for anyone who doesn't have autonomy and can't keep it together always. I looked hard at the road and considered my options. I would at least attempt to forge this path. I didn't think about the finish line. Remember the poem I have hanging in my office? Frost's "The Road Not Taken." It always leaves me thinking how readers interpret it as a vague poem. He clearly says, "I took the road less travelled by, and that has made all the difference." Some of my students had argued with me that the difference he speaks of is melancholic, a loss, something that he cannot take back. But what is actually retrievable from our experiences? What is not worthy of grieving, even the moment of pleasure that passes, the success that comes after a long journey? The "difference" for me is always in the attempt. I would rather the experimental error, but at least I would have hypothesised.

But enough with my circular notions and let me

say that I was still privileged because I had the financial support to study abroad. Both of my parents did all that they could, and my grand-uncle who I reached out to for support helped fund me because he believed in education. His Palestinian blood believed only in education, never the home, the body, the state of belonging. He had once explained to me that "diaspora" was nothing more than grand theory labelling a state that Palestinians had always known. He argued that even if I had a home, and I was only "half" Palestinian, I would always carry pulsating diaspora in my veins, like a blood type, something you couldn't get away from. Except I felt that the state of diaspora and exile was from the land of the healthy. I was constantly in the land of the sick and I didn't know if I would ever return to my first homeland.

o

I was not alone when I pursued my graduate study. One of my good friends, Hannah, was also considering her graduate degree abroad. Her family also believed in the power of education. They were hesitant about a degree in literature, but she convinced them she would excel in it and still return home. The main rule was to return home. There would be no escaping the traditional home. Hannah and I were very similar in our love for literature and our desire to make a difference in the world. She wanted to teach, just like me. She wanted to think about ways that women could be treated as real equals in society, and she hoped that a degree would grant her a sense of strength that she struggled to find back home. Having Hannah travel with me eased my mother's worries. Hannah was loving, responsible, and more than anything, she was the daughter of medical doctors, and understood what living with MS meant. I was comfortable living with Hannah and felt that someone was around to witness this part of my life's journey. Having someone witness your life is not a feeling that can be described in limited words. There is no function to witnessing your life except that it reassures you that you are seen, heard, and that you were really there. We took every step together, and each step felt lighter for me because of it. When we first got on the plane to travel to England, I turned to look at her and saw her sobbing. Her body was convulsing and I couldn't understand why she was crying. She dried her tears and smiled at me, explaining that being away from home felt scary, because her parents were old, and she didn't want to leave them behind even for a short while. Hannah was attached to her mother and felt a sense of responsibility towards her. She feared that something would happen to her mother and that it would take Hannah forever to get back home. We simply had to take the risk together, I assured her, and told her that I feared waking up paralysed and unable to move every day, and yet I didn't want to miss out on any part of life. Going abroad for my degree was a risk I was willing to take because I wanted to believe there was light at the end of the tunnel.

But I cried for two days when I woke up in a bed that wasn't my own and looked out of the window to hear seagulls that I didn't know existed in the real world. I thought everything about England was fictional. Surreal. Nothing that I could touch. Even when the snow first hit my face and I screamed in both terror and joy; I didn't think it was real. I was someone who didn't experience the environment but tried to survive it. The cold weather wreaked havoc on my bones and my body suffered as it tried to adjust. But I couldn't adjust and kept calling my mother internationally (she wouldn't use Skype, no matter how many times I tried to teach her). Mama would repeat, "Stay strong. It's not a punishment. This is your road. One day you'll look back and think, I did it! Just like how we learned to read together. Now you need to keep reading. And you are in England! The land of Shakespeare and all the good English stuff you love. There is nothing here. I don't want you to even think of coming back before you're done. No visits."

Mama had to push against my nagging. I had been so persistent, but now that I had landed where I wanted to be, I found the loneliness dreary, isolating, and too painful to survive. I wasn't mad anymore. I was looking for an excuse to return home, but Mama wouldn't have it. And I feared disappointing her, as always. Her voice on the phone strengthened me, like a dose of medication I would take to help me walk faster. And I did just that. I pushed past the homesickness and the desire to be in bed with my dog, Flake. I wanted to return home, but Mama was the gatekeeper who refused to let me back in. Hannah, too, kept stressing that studying abroad was a privilege few people had and that it would be a shame to just throw it all away.

Within two months, I was settled and used to the cold and found that it helped ease some of my heat-induced symptoms. I can't say anything highly interesting happened during my master's studies. I kept my head low, focused on my reading, spoke to Mama on the phone, and waited for the time to pass. Slowly, I began noticing how in my classes I would often be asked to speak about "the Palestinian issue" and defend Islam. In every seminar room, bodies turned to look at me and waited for me to speak. My voice would shake, and I would struggle to speak on behalf of the entire Arab world. Hannah would never be asked the same question. She was always treated differently because she had lighter skin, blonde hair, and green eyes that flashed at you. We quickly noticed that we would be treated differently if she spoke instead of me. At grocery stores, people smiled at her and frowned at me. At the bank, the bankers spoke to me slowly, enunciating every word, while they gave her the typical "hiya" and a smile. In the classes that we took together, our colleagues approached her for outings, coffees, drinks, while they eyed me warily. Only when Hannah would assert that I was her friend and nudge me closer would people try to warm up to me. Hannah quickly noticed the way I was treated, and it started bothering her more than it bothered me. I was used to being treated as though I was invisible everywhere, but she found it strange and shuddered at the thought of any implicit prejudices. We quickly learned new terminology in school and understood the concept of "passing" as one of a certain group, even when you don't really belong with them. She was not the Other like I was, and we observed how even a simple order at a restaurant would go smoother if she was the one speaking. She had the same accent as I did, but people didn't seem to mind. When I spoke, all I heard was "sorry?" and "pardon me?" while all I thought of was how simple my request was. I began fearing speech even more than back home when slurred speech was the issue.

Whenever I used the elevator at school, I received suspicious looks from anyone walking in the hallway. Once, someone I didn't know came up to me and explained that the sign on the elevator meant it was only for disabled people. I nodded and couldn't say a word. Hannah jumped in and said that I was disabled and that we would appreciate if everyone minded their own business. I looked at her and wondered what it would be like to answer back so confidently. On trains and buses, I would look at the seats reserved for the elderly and disabled people and stare at them. I couldn't sit down fearing more harassment. Hannah and I would stand and she would keep telling me to sit down but I just couldn't bring myself to do it. Once, I was exhausted from all the walking and just plopped myself down on a bus seat. At the second bus stop, a middle-aged British woman headed straight for me and asked me to get up.

"The sign says disabled people," she said, as she pointed her cane at me.

I obliged quickly, feeling ashamed of myself. It wasn't worth the public humiliation. Hannah's eyes widened as I moved over to where she was standing and she spoke to me in Arabic, scolding me for letting go of my rights so easily.

"You and her are the same! Don't let anyone treat you that way!" she hissed.

"Khalas! I'm not. She's old. She's got her cane. I don't want to explain anything to her," I replied, unable to look at Hannah and fearing that the woman could understand Arabic. I could still feel her eyes on us.

"I think you really need to carry some sort of sign that says 'I'm disabled too,'" Hannah said, shaking her head.

It was the same everywhere we went. Rejection.

One day, towards the end of our stay in England, there was a severe storm that left us both drowning in wet clothes and we had to take the bus again. We didn't know how to dress for English weather and didn't know what to expect. It had been a sunny morning, but things can change in a nanosecond with the weather's mood swings. I struggled to climb up the bus's stairs and Hannah held my hand for balance. She urged me to sit in the front seats again and I refused, so she did it instead.

"If someone says anything, I'll just say I have a disability," she said.

And I don't know if it was a twist of fate, luck being on her side, or her face that allowed her to sit there. Nobody approached her. It was an experiment that we didn't have the answers to. When we finally got back to our apartment, I took the garbage out before even taking my clothes off. I wanted to stay in the cold because I couldn't sit with my thoughts. Even carrying the garbage bag made me think about its weight in my hands. Everything was hard here. It was just a matter of time until we'd be able to go back home.

There was nothing remarkable about my MA studies except that it was the first step into the journey outside myself and into academia. After completing the degree successfully, I wondered whether a PhD would be feasible. Hannah felt the same way, and we continued the journey together. She was about to get engaged but put off her engagement until she could at least start her first year. Our lives didn't change much. The weather was the same, the treatment we received was the same, and I still felt exhausted just existing. Nothing changed until I started my PhD and met Stella, one of my supervisors. And yes, I know, I am jumping forward in time. There are periods of time when our lives are stagnant and I was waiting for a spark to ignite the next phase of my life.

My PhD topic revolved around madness in literature. What makes women go mad? Do they feign madness? Is madness always real? Those were my initial questions, and like a curious child, I headed into a serious PhD program at another school in the UK, where I hoped to find answers. Chaucer's *Canterbury Tales* revolves around a pilgrimage to Canterbury in Kent, and in a way, I was on the same pilgrimage. I wanted to undertake a steep dive and find greater solace and meaning in literature. It was an all-consuming addiction, and I had just started. And even while beginning this journey I was not preoccupied with the end-game, what happens after the journey is over. It didn't concern me because I believed a PhD would only be a short break from reality, a place where I got to tumble down the rabbit hole, just like Alice.

Alice's Adventures in Wonderland had been a story that my mother often referenced as a warning against escapism. Alice's tears were too big for her. Alice was too small for adults. Alice grew too big. Alice couldn't face her issues. But for me it became a text that dealt with inferiority and how we try to prove ourselves as worthy in the adult world, the world that keeps us always at bay, unless we aim for perfection. Alice wasn't taken seriously even though she was pretty, healthy, witty and daring. But at least she got her adventures. She played with other creatures and forged a narrative for herself. I believed I deserved my own narrative. My father started telling me I was straying too far off from normalcy, from a social life, from the possibility of having my own family. "Too much of something isn't good for you," he would say. My aunts agreed with him, scoffing at the possibility of a degree that took too much time, and particularly one where I was studying madness? And I wasn't an actual doctor? How privileged, how much time-wasting, how irresponsible. The remarks went on and my mother had to bear the weight of them. She insisted that because I was the first in the tribe to pursue a higher degree, I would face the most scrutiny and criticism.

Throughout the years of studying, I remained constantly aware that the clock was ticking, that time was running out, and that I just had to get closer to the finish line. Living with a disability had put me in a different time zone from everyone around me. It's like time itself is crippled, broken, disabled. I experienced time differently: it was either too slow, too fast, or hard to read. I couldn't tell when my body would give out. I couldn't tell when I would have to fight to get out of bed, or when my eyelids would grow heavier and stop me from reading the fine print in front of me. I would curl up in a ball and just wish time would release me from its grip and send me back home. When I started falling behind in my reading and writing, I felt I had to tell one of my supervisors. I had been assigned two supervisors, as is the case with all PhD students. One supervisor was older, a full professor, polished and rusted by academia. The second was young, fresh-blooded, ready to take on academia and create a name for herself. I was nervous around her because she was so articulate and never had to pause to gather her thoughts. I admired her ability to blend so well with British culture although she was Greek. I felt closer to her because she was not *one of them*, and yet not Arab like me. She was the mediator between me and a very white culture that left me constantly stuttering and hesitant. I was still learning to voice my opinions and learning how to say no to suggestions I didn't feel I wanted to take up.

I was careful with the way I interacted with my supervisors because I had struggled during my MA program with condescending remarks that left me unsure about my ability to finish the program.

Rumour had it that most people dropped out from the insane pressure and academic bullying. If you had a supervisor who bullied you, you were most likely to crack under pressure. Comments such as "This is not good enough" and "PhDs aren't for everyone, you know" were common. Some people were told they were too young to be in a PhD program and others were too old. Nothing was just right. Hannah felt the same, constantly being told that she should move to the UK and embark on a serious career path that would take her places rather than return home. When she mentioned she had marriage plans and wanted to start a family instead of working in academia, she was met with frowns and disappointment. Slowly, I started understanding that academia was not a world of possibilities but a world where the strong-minded and strong-willed last. Not everyone would commit to staying the course. So, I stayed the course only because I was curious to see how far along I could get and how long I would last.

Growing up, I remember a character called Curious George. A monkey who would always get in trouble, curiosity was his tragic flaw, but also the driving force behind the entire series of events that makes up his narrative. George's curiosity is both playful and troubling. But the books teach us about forgiveness (self-forgiveness being key), and the ability to start over after every failed attempt. As much as the title seems to indicate that George's curiosity constantly gets him into trouble, we are attached to his character's desire to explore the world and are always rooting for him. The books rely on humour throughout the narrative; even when he falls and hits his head somewhere, this is humorous to him. I now think that humour and playfulness are the key ingredients to unsurpassable difficulties, especially those that are our own doings and failings. When I read the word "lame" scrawled all over the first chapter of my thesis, the words attacked my throat and burned my eyes. I nearly choked. And then I remembered laughing at Curious George while reading about his adventures and began to smile. My smile quickly turned into laughter as I held the pages in my hands and thought about the word's intended usage. Lame. Lame as in crippled? Lame as in uninteresting, small, ineffective. Meant to be a disappointment, an almost. It was weak. Weakened by the multiplicity of scholars' voices crowding my own thoughts and making my voice barely audible. I was repeating words, swirling them around on the page, spitting them out and calling it whole. I embarked on my thesis writing journey expecting twists and turns, bumps and holes, but never to consider myself maimed.

After that first major bump in my path, I relaxed into the writing process and imagined the words as mine amidst a polyphony of voices. I thought of my writing as different with its grammatical errors, lapses of language, and English as my adopted mother tongue. It was bound to be imperfect and erroneous. It was a zone of unclear borders for me. I would think in Arabic and English but have to write in English. I would get mad in Arabic and curse in English. I would respond politely in English to comments on my paper but delete my "ya'ateek al-afyah" at the end of the email. But it was always there in my head, even if not having its home in text. Writing in English, I felt like a trespasser, like someone who wasn't expected to write in English. Comments like "But this is really good for a non-native speaker" made me think I was happy to be a non-native speaker. Until I started recognising that these words were not meant to be complimenting and flattering. What of all others who were not welcomed into the language? They were sent to academic writing centres, like a boot camp for Others Wanting to Write in English. I didn't get sent to one because my errors were fixable with a few dashes and pinches. I realised that in this acceptance, I was also "passing," just like Hannah had earlier. Our experiences were different but still similar. I struggled with excessive fatigue and strained to keep my eyes open, and Hannah helped me read some of the material and urged me to keep going. I had never felt as accepted as in that moment when she told me I didn't need good eyesight to read, that there were always ways around any obstacles, and if there weren't enough ways, then she would be there to help guide me. I was still ashamed of my body's failures and didn't want to depend on anyone, but I struggled to find accessible books with large print and audiobooks weren't always available, especially for scholarly work. I remember one of the first books that Stella mentioned to me. She suggested far too many books and too many titles that I could barely keep up. But she introduced me first to Nancy Mairs, who writes of her experience with MS in *Carnal Acts*. When I first read Mairs's work, I tried to make sense of the feelings of shame which were suddenly replaced by—dare I say it—pride. I was proud to be connected in some way to Nancy Mairs, the writer, this woman who was reclaiming her womanhood, her disability, her "voice" as she so elegantly puts it. Mairs's work spoke to me on many levels. She could describe the experience of having MS in a way that no medical terminology had managed to do, and no neurologist had taken the time to explain to me. I have some of her passages jotted everywhere in my notebooks.

> *Living with this mysterious mechanism feels like*
> *having your present self, and the past selves it embod-*
> *ies, haunted by a capricious and meanspirited ghost,*
> *unseen except for its footprints, which trips you even*
> *when you're watching where you're going . . . and*
> *weights your whole body with a weariness no amount*
> *of rest can relieve. An alien invader must be at work.*
> *But, of course, it's not. It's your own body. That is, it's*
> *you.* (Carnal Acts)

MS, then, almost seems non-existent. A ghost that attacks your body. Because it is my body which has somehow decided to plot against my corporeal self, my ethereal self, and my self-image is shaken. This "self" of mine is called into question. How am I to come to terms with the fact that I must succumb to the will of the body, when culture has always suggested that the power of the mind is endless? MS itself originates in the mind and its extensions, the central nervous system, the greatest powerhouse, yet it manifests itself mainly as bodily symptoms. The mind destroys the body, or is it the body that is destroying the mind? I didn't have the answers, but Stella provided me with the right questions to ask. As a mentor, she began asking me what it felt like to live within my body. Stella started explaining to me what accessibility meant, that I had the right to ask for more time, for extensions with deadlines, that I had the right to be listened to.

To be listened to when you're a woman is a frustrating process. There are always others willing to jump in and speak for you, speak on your behalf, help you speak, claim you don't know how to speak so they will do it for you. As a woman with disability, it becomes even harder to be listened to. People assume you have a shameful body simply because you are a woman, you walk around with your 'awra, a voice that has to be concealed, veiled, silenced. The disabled body is also meant to be hidden, clothed in shame, remaining unrevealed to others because of its grotesqueness, its crossing of boundaries. It is a body that calls attention to itself even when it is meant to be hidden behind closed doors. As I read more about disability literature, I walked through the forest of illness narratives and started tracing footsteps of authors who had experienced bouts of illnesses or who were disabled. They had voices that were often muffled and unheard, and yet I had not attempted to listen to their illness narratives. I did not know that centuries ago, the great Virginia Woolf had penned her essay on illness which she aptly titled "On Being Ill."

As a literature scholar at the time, I had read Woolf's *Mrs. Dalloway*, *Orlando*, and my all-time favourite, *A Room of One's Own*. All through my years of poring over literary passages written by her, I had adopted the idea that women needed to claim their own space (whether by occupying a room of their own, space in society, or claiming their voices). I had understood that women needed to flourish and grow, but would be able to do so only if there were certain environmental and societal factors helping this growth. I had considered time and space, both linear and non-linear, and the way that Mrs. Dalloway says "she would buy the flowers herself."

o

For more than fifteen years, I have been thinking about Mrs. Dalloway's flowers. That's the opening line of the novel, you remember, how many times I asked you to underline it, how many times I emphasised the flowers, and what the act of buying your own flowers could possibly do for a woman like Mrs. Dalloway, like me, and like you.

So, Yasmeen, a woman has to have her own space, has to buy her own flowers, has to be able to bend the rules and think of society as "everything and nothing"—society makes the rules for her to live by and yet society is nothing but ash in Orlando's reality. If Woolf was observing and commenting on women's lives and creating characters who used language to sharpen their tongues, what would happen to women who fall ill and have no language to speak in? Woolf answered my anxieties when she mused over the failures of society, literature and language in providing a mirror for the ill body:

> *Considering how common illness is, how tremendous the spiritual change that it brings, how astonishing, when the lights of health go down, the undiscovered countries that are then disclosed, what wastes and deserts of the soul a slight attack of influenza brings to light, what precipices and lawns sprinkled with bright flowers a little rise of temperature reveals, what ancient and obdurate oaks are uprooted in us in the act of sickness, how we go down into the pit of death and feel the waters of annihilation close above our head . . . it becomes strange indeed that illness has not taken its place with love, battle, and jealousy among the prime themes of literature. ("On Being Ill")*

I wanted literature to save me from living within my body, and yet as I escaped into my close-reading annotation of my literary texts, I wondered why I didn't know that literary greats like Woolf, Franz Kafka, Albert Camus, Emily Dickinson, Fyodor Dostoyevsky had struggled with illness and had written about it. Throughout my entire undergraduate career and postgraduate years, I thought all of my favourite authors were perfect and ethereal creatures, never having experienced illness or disability. I thought that their personal lives hadn't been touched by bodily suffering and that they sometimes experienced bouts of depression that only fuelled their writing. Because I had been focusing on how madness is presented in literary texts, I had somehow believed that the mind was worth writing about, exploring, dissecting, but never the body. I was sure that bodies were secondary, that the mind was always more graceful and worth respecting. Growing up, we are told that the mind is one of God's many gifts to us, a blessing, one that "separates" us from animals. This rhetoric is also problematic for me because it elevates human beings over other creatures that haven't been blessed with our beautiful mind mazes. But one tiny fracture in one of these inextricably connected nerves and we lose our way and are reduced to failing bodies. As I thought about all my lovely madwomen protagonists, I tried to find a common link. Something that clicked for me, a thread that connected all these fictional characters experiencing the fictional repercussions of mental illness.

Annihilation. Complete and utter annihilation. That's what happens at the end of all the narratives. Bertha Mason, my madwoman in the attic, ends up setting fire to Thornfield Hall and throwing herself off the roof in *Jane Eyre*—a novel that doesn't even grant Bertha a voice and reduces her to a creature crawling "on all fours." There are too many other protagonists like Bertha, shoved somewhere, hidden in an attic, a basement, a room, a tent, or completely self-annihilated. That's how it all begins. Repression by a patriarchal society, women's bodies are controlled and regulated, told how to behave, what to wear, how to speak, who to love, who to unlove, and how to breathe, how to die. Corsets that wrap around your waist, reaching up to your lungs, slowly sucking the air out of you, depriving you of oxygen that your mind needs. What happens? Tragic heroines. Women who throw themselves under a train after being ostracised for too long, women who pay the price for daring to speak.

"They lose their mind, Professor. Something so precious," Yasmeen comments, stating the obvious. But I pick up on the loss.

"To lose something means you have always had it as ultimately whole and yours. We believe in the wholeness of the human mind, the body, and the spirit. And you say precious because you, too, believe in its value," I respond, reiterating as I used to do in class.

Do we really fully own our minds and our thoughts and the way we choose to go about our lives? We lose a fragment every day, a minuscule piece gets splintered off. We lose a small part of ourselves and our minds develop scars the way that MS patients' minds develop lesions that interrupt our communication pathways. The scars cause lapses in our minds, our memories, and we end up losing our minds, our selves, like Cathy in *Wuthering Heights* who severs herself from her soulmate Heathcliff because society says she can't marry a "gypsy." So, Cathy twists herself inside out and stretches her body to fit into British society and marries Edgar Linton, the man who fits all the accepted boxes, but doesn't quite fit her body. Cathy, a tragic heroine who existed in nineteenth-century British literary imagination, was not too different from the women in my life and women I had heard of.

As I became more invested in literary heroines, I began to see many Cathys and Berthas around me. I remembered growing up with the story my mother used to narrate, the one about their neighbour's cousin. She was a lovely and bright girl, Shireen, with long black hair, hazel eyes that pierced you. Shireen was in love with Mahmood for so long, almost obsessively so. She married him when she was eighteen, as soon as she graduated from high school. After she married Mahmood, he didn't allow her to pursue her university degree. She had one of the highest GPAs in the country and wanted so badly to go to medical school. She was a scientist, one who experimented with oil and salt and water in the kitchen, turning her mother's tiny kitchen into a laboratory for her theories and hypotheses. And she was also very pretty. The whole neighbourhood swore that her eyes were deep pools that drew you in, her hair draped around her like an expensive winter shawl, and her friendly demeanour welcomed everyone, young and old. But her father had always said she would become a doctor, the first in her family to do so, their Palestinian blood having produced male doctors and engineers, but no girls had trodden that path yet. She would be the first.

But Shireen was not the first doctor. Shireen married Mahmood and was the first to end up in a medical institution—not as a doctor, but as a patient suffering from unexplained bouts of mania. After starting her life with Mahmood, she lost her beauty, by all accounts. He was busy at school, studying, growing older, smarter, sharper, and more polished, while she stayed at home polishing his shoes, preparing his ties for class, and then supporting him through graduate school as he became a professor of chemistry. As Mahmood grew into himself, he stopped seeing Shireen. She gained so much weight that she was unrecognisable. She threw away all the mirrors at home and hated her children's clinginess. She would hate him too, eventually asking for a divorce. But he wouldn't let her go because he feared his father and hers. He kept her close by, on a leash, with no access to the outside world, as she got sicker. He refused to seek help because he was a man who worried about his social status and reputation. He didn't want people to know he had a mad wife. And so, Shireen's condition worsened, until she tried to suffocate one of her children, the girl. "The one that looked like her," Mama said, repeating the story told to her. I never understood why it was the girl who Shireen chose to suffocate. Did she choose to? Did she hate her? Was she saving her somehow? Mama would shake her head at me, stating that there are no mothers that kill. It didn't happen.

Shireen's daughter survived, but Shireen was thrown back to her father and mother, who couldn't take care of her. They were ageing and had no means to understand what was happening to their beautiful mad daughter. She would wash herself obsessively, pouring antiseptic solutions over her milky skin, scrubbing herself and repeating Mahmood's name. The only other word she said was "why" . . . why what? I don't know. But I do know that Shireen's story stayed with me as I searched for answers to every breakdown I read about and every narrative I tried to decipher. What happened to Shireen's mother and daughter? Where were they in her narrative? They went on with their lives, and her mother went on to her death, while Shireen remained locked up, heavily medicated, not able to remember that she had three children. Her children were my age now, and they had moved on to start their own careers and raise their own families. I don't know if her daughter ever recovered from her mother's attempted suffocation of her, but I have a hunch that she never recovered from her mother's wounds. Mothers who kill are still mothers. Mothers who bleed onto you are still mothers. Mothers who don't remember you are still mothers. Just like a country that goes up in flames is still your home, even if nothing remains.

We don't just lose parts of ourselves, we don't just lose our minds, but we lose familial bonds, our roots are severed and trees begin to grow elsewhere. I wrote and rewrote the title to my thesis, I thought about a breakdown as a breakthrough, an exit from society's imprisonment of women. What if madness was the way out? What if freedom really meant losing it all? In the Sufi tradition, the closest level to God is Baqaa, a state of life with God, through God, in God, and for God. But before that stage is reached, the most difficult part is Fanaa. Complete annihilation of the self, the ego, our desire for materialism, our desire for desire itself. What if exiting society was a way to reclaim the lost parts of yourself, even if it meant losing your mind?

But this was too troublesome and would get me in trouble with academics. I wasn't advocating for suicide. I wasn't saying that to break down meant to successfully work through the muddiness and finally break through. I was wondering whether breakdowns and breakthroughs were interconnected, whether the light at the end of the tunnel was actually the bright light I saw when I died, whether the light was just the welcoming embrace of a better place? Breakdowns are places of breakage, carnage, ruptures. Sometimes the breakthrough is a narrative that does not end, but a story that continues with others telling the story of the loss. It is the loss that remains, lingering outside the text, and the shards sting our skin. We read about these tragic heroines, we listen to the stories handed down to us by neighbours, mothers, grandmothers, and we think of ways to amend the narrative. Change the story. Change the ending. Even a tragic death or descent into madness is something worth contemplating, a seed worth planting, a story worth rewriting.

"I think there's agency in these narratives, Professor. I remember the word agency and trying to understand it in class. You kept asking us if we had any agency and I didn't know where I could get some of that," Yasmeen comments, a twinkle in her eye as she retrieves a distant, much alive memory.

Agency is closely linked to the body you're born into, the home you grow up in, the country that rears you. To have just a semblance of agency over your own life is a blessing gone unnoticed. So many times, we think we have agency, but we misread the social structures at work that undermine our ability to have autonomy over our own bodies and lives. It's like the phrase you and your friends say to each other: "You go, girl!" You are applauding the ability to make your own choices as women, and you are both driven and inspired by those who do. It's what all the feminists have called for—and I won't get into all the different types and waves of feminism with you, but I know you remember. Mary Wollstonecraft started with her calling for the rights of women and Simone de Beauvoir picked up with her "one is not born but rather becomes a woman" statement, and this stretches to other feminists and women writers. So, we are all in a constant state of becoming agents of resistance to oppression and leading autonomous lives, even when we simply shake our heads in a defiant "no." It's the right to think your own thoughts, the power to ask for a choice before even making one, the ability to

recognise that the narrative must be written by you—
the one who is told to lower her voice, the one who
disappears from the narrative early on, the one who
is set aside, always on the margins. Pushing against
these margins gives us agency. You push a little, and
then a little more, and then you get closer to the finish
line.

"And you got your PhD, so you got to the finish
line. Did it feel like the finish line? Did you hear the
applause in your head?"

o

I don't know if I heard applause, but I remember the
three-hour viva stretching out until I could not feel my
tongue in my mouth. I imagine Sylvia Plath saying, "The
tongue stuck in my jaw. // It stuck in a barb wire snare.
/ Ich, ich, ich, ich." Plath couldn't talk to her father out
of fear and her very toxic relationship with him, but it's
this idea of voice that I'm interested in. She tries to get
the words out but they don't come, instead, she stutters
and stammers and trips over her words. During my
viva examination, I sat in the wooden chair, uncomfortable, sweating, wearing a chequered grey blazer to
look formal, hair tied back, serious. Two male professors had read my thesis and asked me questions and as
the great traditions of academia go, I was to defend my
work, say it was worthwhile, worth being referred to as
a reference, a great addition to the canon of academic
scholarship on literature. Were my words worthy of the
badge of honour that I would carry, would I be deserv-
ing of being knighted?

I noticed the clock ticking behind the well-
accomplished professor's head and started losing my
vision slowly. Blurry eights or sixes. What did it matter?

I just wanted to stretch my muscles, rub my eyes, yawn freely, roll my shoulders back to relieve the spasms. I asked for a five-minute break but the lead examiner refused, asking me to wait just a little bit. And I waited, squirming in my seat, my body retaliating, asking to be released. I imagined barbed wire tying me securely to the chair and focused my vision on the professor's moustache as he mouthed yet another question based on his reading of page one-hundred-something. I tried to keep my neck in place as it was refusing to help me hold my head up. I just wanted it to cooperate until we finished the exam.

The questions went on and I tried to admit that there was more work to be done, always. Stella had reminded me to be humble, to remember that a PhD is a terminal degree, but that doesn't mean you should present yourself as a know-it-all. "There's always room for improvement," she would say, and I would nod, trying to remember her words and put them into practice. If there was truly a finish line, shouldn't the work stop? I only wanted to get close to the finish line, never really finish. Eternal student syndrome, perhaps. But I finally saw the lead examiner get up, and the external examiner follow his movement. They both walked towards me and I got up, hoping that I had read the cue correctly.

"We don't usually let you know immediately, but you have been looking unwell for the past few hours, noticeably so. So, we will just share the news," the grey-haired professor said, and added, "You are now officially Dr. Alshammari." He stuck his hand out to shake mine.

And what a moment that was, holding on to his hand for balance, shaking it for formality, and feeling my limbs struggle to connect, my brain cells processing his voice, his facial cues, and reminding myself to speak.

"Thank you, thank you, Professor! I don't know what to say!" I exclaimed, my voice barely audible. It was as though I had whispered in his ear but heard myself scream.

"I guess you can take your five-minute break now and come back in for technicalities after," he responded, smiling gently, and looking at his colleague who extended his hand to congratulate me, too.

I walked out of that office and texted my mother and father the same message: Done.

When I was outside, facing the School of English, I took a deep breath and knelt down to stretch. I raised my arms, facing the sky, and freed my arms from the imaginary handcuffs. Oxygen filled my lungs and I shivered in the cold British air, October 31st, Halloween, where everyone dresses up and goes on a scare. Here I was, a postgraduate, a doctor, and I was all dressed up for the role. What a ride, I thought, and at that moment, I didn't think there would be more. I really was done. But my father wasn't done. He printed three hundred copies of my thesis, hard-bound, black, with fine gold print titling each copy. Gold, he said, just like me. I was goldened by the degree, in his eyes. He stacked my closet with them, shelves of a reminder that this was me, written into the days of research, my closet always warmly holding my memories of an era I can no longer imagine was mine.

o

"But this is my work behind you, lined up like the vertebrae that hold me up, except the gold is somewhat abrased," I say, breathing in the nostalgic air.

139

Four

Chapter F of Four

Diary Entry: "It's hard to watch my students struggle with so much and still be detached from them. What are the rules of being a good teacher? How do I help them when I can barely walk? What do I do to make their lives more bearable? I'm finally a doctor. But who cares? In the grand scheme of things, who really cares?"

Time and desire are strange concepts. We want things so badly, and with time, we want other things. We crave the torment of not having gotten what we wanted, and the tortured artist is a great example of this level of commitment to art. It tips back and forth between bouts of creativity and productivity and, on the other hand, bouts of hopelessness and despair. Virginia Woolf, Ernest Hemingway, Sylvia Plath, Vincent van Gogh, Frida Kahlo, all of them had periods of great outpouring of artistic genius and with that same creativity found creative ways to exit life. Frida Kahlo, in one of her famous diary entries, says: *I hope the exit is joyful. And I hope never to return . . . Painting completed my life.* Plath wrote her semi-autobiographical novel *The Bell Jar* and ended her life a month after its publication. So, success and reaching the finish line had nothing to do with their desire to continue, to go on. Is every creative genius stricken by madness? Do we always need some sort of reason to stay alive, to push, to persevere? How do we stay rooted when we can so quickly slide to the darkness? I struggled with thoughts of hopelessness as I got worse physically but had now become who I envisioned myself to be. My surgical experiment had not worked, had not stopped the disease from progressing, but it seemed to have at least reduced my symptoms. I was still struggling with immense fatigue and my limbs were always too heavy for me. I had balance issues and struggled to keep my head up, my feet in the right positions. But still, I had the doctorate in hand and was ready to take on the world.

"In my head, you've always been you—a teacher, a good one. Never did I imagine you as having any issues. I just saw you as strong, successful, someone I wanted to be exactly like. It's strange to read this entry and think that you ever doubted yourself," Yasmeen says.

That's the way we look at mothers, too. We look at mothers as the place where we left but always want to return to. We instinctively know that safety is within the womb, that we will always be cared for by the one who knows what to do when times get tough. It's how I felt about my mother, but also how I felt about the good teachers I had. I couldn't imagine that Stella was anything less than perfect. I also had Dr. Wafaa, who taught me during my undergraduate years and introduced me to the basics of critical theory. Dr. Wafaa was the type of professor who believed in establishing friendships with her students. She would have us all sit in a circle, every day, for every lecture. She refused to lecture at the front of the room, saying she didn't want to be the one feeding us information. She didn't want to be the all-knowing one, she would say, shrugging her shoulders as if saying she did know it all but didn't want to appear aloof or superior.

I remember that even after I graduated and later

taught my own classes, I went to Wafaa (she insisted we call her by her first name, even when we were her students), and asked her for advice. I had a notebook in hand and wanted to listen to her and she smiled at me, coffee mug in hand, telling me that there was no one way to teach. But there were things to keep in mind. You had to be honest. You had to be transparent. You had to remember where you came from, how you got here, the time it took for you to arrive at your destination. You had to remember your students' names, even if you had a poor memory. You had to show up. No matter what, you had to show up.

"Don't get lazy. Don't slack off," Wafaa would say.

The words still ring in my head and the unintentional pressure that comes with those words is hard to ignore. I tried to stay focused and give my classes my all. I think that academia is experienced differently for female faculty members. Women are seen as more welcoming and nurturing than men, and I find that students tend to gravitate more towards their teachers when they're women. But it took me many years to consider the emotional labour that we do as women. We form friendships with our students and listen to their stories and exchange energies with them all the time. I became one of those teachers for you and others. My memory is filled with faces and names that have been seated in front of me as I lectured, and bodies that sat across from me in my office, spilling their secrets and fears, reaching out to me for support amidst the chaos.

I must have taught thousands and thousands of students. Each semester has a fond memory for me, but it becomes endlessly maddening to attempt to capture its essence again, to remember the literary texts that I taught. But I'll go through the fragments, the ones that helped me learn the most about how we interact with others on a daily basis and how we are touched by these lives. Academia for me was the product of a politics of love. Love and only love. Emotional labour did not feel like labour to me. But it felt like giving birth to others, slowly, gently, reaching out towards them, granting them my time, energy, and love, only to see them grow slowly into what they wanted to become. Teaching became the lifeline that I held on to and the lifelines on my palms resembled my teaching career.

o

My first job was at a university that functioned more as a community college, with students from all age groups, different backgrounds, but less privileged and with less access to traditional education. The university followed an open-learning program, which meant the students interacted less with the professors and did more self-paced learning. I was excited to teach at the university and make a difference in their lives. My head of department assigned me my first class: Renaissance Literature and Shakespearean Drama. She was slightly concerned because it was an all-male class. She raised an eyebrow at me, asking me if I felt comfortable with that. I shifted my feet uncomfortably in her office, worried about the male/female power dynamic, and yet I lied blatantly and said that I did not mind *at all*. She let me know that many of them were actually older than me and that they would struggle with a woman professor. They had been taught solely by male professors and this would be new for them.

"It will take them a bit of time to adjust to you," Dr. Carole said. She was both calming me down and making me more anxious about these mysterious students.

"I'm very professional, I can handle it," I said, shifting my weight to my left side and moving my cane swiftly to my right hand. Her eyes landed on the cane and blinked excessively.

"I believe I can recognise a star when I see one," she professed, adding, "so good luck. I'm here if there's major trouble, but otherwise you will be fine."

I was assigned to the male class but I also had an all-female class. They were segregated not just in classrooms but in buildings. Whenever I crossed over into the male building, the security guards followed me not-so-subtly, almost worrying about having a female presence onsite. I always made sure I looked sharp and professional, a long blazer covering my body and loose pants allowing me freer movement as I walked to classes with my cane and leather messenger bag over my shoulder, its weight pressing heavily on me. My books were always at least six hundred pages long, fine print, difficult to read, but even more so, difficult to carry. By the time I walked into my 7 pm lecture, I was sleepy and fatigued, my body losing its energy, my legs feeling like they were fighting through layers of mud. I had no choice; the class was at 7 pm to allow working students to finish work, go home to their families and children, and come to class much later in the evening. Young men registered for the 7 pm class while young women were slotted for the 5 pm class, a bit earlier, since many of them were married and had to be home with their children and husbands. Many of the women didn't drive and would have male family members come to pick them up from campus (brothers, fathers, or husbands). I could see that many of the students struggled to come to campus, and yet most of the class showed up. Absences were hardly an issue. They almost always wanted to be in class. For them, having access to education was a privilege. Most of the students would save money in order to pay their tuition.

Sometimes the entire extended family would chip in for one student's fees; uncles, aunts, grandparents, neighbours, strangers from the same tribe would all contribute. This is when I realised how much a collective society could be a privilege and that it was not always oppressive. Everyone would work together to support the one who needed the most help. There wouldn't be any hesitation. If the young man was bright, the entire family would help him get through school. If the young woman was self-motivated, the mother figure would push the father and other males in the family to support her education. I listened to these stories as I got to know my students and understood that they did not have it as easy as the rest of the world believed. They weren't spoiled rich Middle Eastern kids. They didn't have oil pumping in their backyards. They were lumped in the same privileged category just because they lived in a wealthy country. But there were specific family circumstances, stories that went unnoticed, students who were citizen-less in their own homes, those who were struggling to build a life for themselves. I began understanding their lives through the literary texts we studied together, and I started guiding them into seeing the connections.

First lectures are always filled with trepidation, no matter where you're positioned, whether you're the authority figure or the student. You don't know what to expect and yet you pretend to be poised. Nervousness is a mixture of butterflies and snakes coiling around your neck, applying pressure on your throat, making it harder for your voice to boom the way it's meant to. Project through the lecture hall and echo. But I couldn't project because my voice grew weaker by 7 pm. I had my water bottle in hand, wetting my lips and asking the water to magically give me energy. When I walked into the big lecture hall, the pale grey walls seemed to look back at me and challenge me to make the room any brighter. I walked in with my "Al-salam-alaikom" and around thirty-five students echoed my greeting in unison, their voices booming louder than any microphone I planned to use. I settled myself at the podium, placing my book and syllabus next to me, ready for me to refer to.

"My name is Dr. Alshammari and this is Renaissance and Shakespeare 204. I hope you're in the right class. We will meet here every Monday and Wednesday at seven sharp, and if I can get here on time, then I'm sure you can," I stated firmly. First lectures are all about setting the tone. Friendliness would come later on during the course, as I let down my armour.

I heard one of the young men scoff and I wasn't sure why. He was sprawled on the seat with his legs open wide and his body language signifying a complete lack of interest. I looked his way to see if I could read him. When I did, he smirked.

"Is there a problem?" I asked, glaring at him. He was a big guy and was too big for the small chair he was sitting in.

"No. It's just weird they brought us a young doctor. A girl, too," he replied, looking at his fellow classmates for support.

"Ah, so there is a problem. Well, you have the choice to stay or not," I replied. "I hold a degree from one of the top schools in the UK. My age makes me good at my job, actually. And in this classroom, gender is not an issue. I'm your professor and you're the student. Girl professor or not, you follow my rules, until you're finished and we never have to see each other again."

He nodded at me and looked the other way while the rest of the young men smiled sheepishly and glanced back at him to check on his reaction. Some students sat up in their seats, and I knew I had gotten their attention. Others folded their arms in anticipation of a difficult professor who was about to bully them. Some smiled at me gently, in what seemed to be a supportive gesture.

I went through the syllabus and explained my rules and my availability for office hours while urging them to keep up with the reading at all times. One of the men in army uniform raised his hand.

"Ma afham englaizi. So, what to do?" he asked, leaning over his chair, folding his arms as he looked at me.

"And you're studying English literature? Why? Why are you even here?" I asked. The class erupted in low, manly giggles.

He shrugged his shoulders and told me it was the only degree that he was interested in. It wasn't science or business, and he was hoping to get better at it. But reading Shakespeare throughout the semester? How did I even expect that of him?

"Shakespeare is difficult to read, yes, and I feel the same most of the time. It sounds like a foreign language to me. But you need to figure out a way to pass the class. Use Google. Use YouTube. Use whatever it takes for the text to make sense to you."

"But you're Arab. You should be more easygoing and not expect much of us," he said.

"I am Arab, but that's exactly why you're lucky to have me. I expect you to be better at this than a native speaker. You will bring your culture to what you read.

Shakespeare isn't just for the British. He's ours, too. And literature and drama are what you do daily. Like right now. This looks to me like a very dramatic scene between two characters who are getting into conflict," I challenged him, walking over to the edge of the room, near the door, "and I wonder who will exit stage first?"

He laughed and denied that he would drop the class, letting me know that he had to stay because he had paid for the entire semester's tuition, adding, "Haram to lose all that money."

The conversation ended there, and I went on to assign Shakespeare's *Othello* as the first reading and explained that it would take up the majority of the semester. I was not a Shakespearean expert by any means, but I was excited to see how Renaissance culture could be read and adapted today to a very tribal culture. Harold Bloom, literary critic, says we don't read Shakespeare, but actually, Shakespeare reads us. What this means is that Shakespeare will appear when the student is ready, and the lessons learned are uncountable. I was just hoping that they would learn to pick up on the intricacies of Shakespearean language but this was not my ultimate goal. I wanted to be able to speak to them about their own biases and prejudices.

At the end of class, I hobbled down the hall with my cane and one student followed me out, calling after me. "Diktorah, Diktorah, salamat!"

I turned around and answered him with the respectful "Allah eysalmik," but didn't know whether to explain to him that this was not a bout of illness he could wish me a speedy recovery from. I could see his gentle eyes glisten and his wrinkles extend as if extending his deepest sympathies. I ended the potential conversation prematurely and said, "See you next class!" The sound of my cane echoed in the empty halls at 9:05 pm, campus preparing to sleep through the night before the bustling 9 am start to the day.

I met my first women's class at 11 am the next morning. I had bursts of energy during the morning, so I was content with the class being scheduled in the morning. I walked into an extremely packed and loud classroom; the image contrasted sharply with the night before. The majority of the young women were covered in black abayas while others were wearing niqabs. When I walked in, I closed the door behind me to let them know it would be just us, no men allowed, and that they should feel comfortable. I also wanted to connect with them more and see their faces so that I could learn their names faster. My memory was often failing me because of my neurons refusing to learn the drill, but I kept trying anyway. Over the years I forget names and my memory replaces these lost ones with other compatible names, except I believe in the importance of our names. Who we are is tied to how our name is pronounced, how it sounds and the tone with which it is articulated. I wanted to keep track of the names one by one and slowly learn who each of them was. I can't say I succeeded, but I fell in love with that class, with its energy, its conversations and side-conversations that I would have to stop, and I started using Arabic and English to explain difficult phrases to them. Only one woman dropped that class after meeting me for the first time. She was extremely uncomfortable with my age, a young twenty-something professor, while she was much older, a grandmother. She flat-out told me she would not be taught by someone from the "younger generation, who didn't know how hard it was to study back in the day." She picked up her bag and books and left the class, not waiting for my response. I looked back at the class and shrugged my shoulders, delving right into the beauty of a literature degree.

"Why are you in my class and what do you hope to learn?" I asked. "I don't want to know the answers verbally. I want to see it in writing. Write me a note. A letter. A short text message and jot it down. I'll collect the papers at the end and see you next class."

With that, the tearing of notebook pages began to annoy my ears and I cringed at every fast slash of the pages. My senses were either too sharp or too far gone, nothing in-between. As I stood facing them while they penned their thoughts and others chewed on their pencils, tempted to play with their phones, I sat myself at the desk, on the short and uncomfortable plastic chair. I considered how different the scene looked from there, seated, waist-high. This gave me a preview of being a disabled teacher, what I would experience in years to come, having to sit rather than walk around the classroom, having to watch my students take their exams as I roll down the hall, peering at their papers alongside them rather than looking at them from above. There would be no professor looming above, there would be the professor wheeling herself beneath you, waist-high in the world. I had once gone to a job interview at a university where I was required to teach the class. That day, I could not stand up, let alone walk. So, I sat through the entire teaching demo, talking to the students with my hands on the desk, holding on to it for balance and posture. The other professor who was meant to evaluate my teaching skills wrote a horrible report, one that highlighted that I was not "engaging" and had no "teacher charisma that would hold a class for long, as she was sitting down the whole time." I didn't get that job, and I did not turn to a lawyer to support my case. I had simply walked away and found myself here. Perhaps that's the thing about fight-or-flight responses. You land somewhere, whether you fight or run off. I was happy with where I ended up, seated across from women who desperately wanted to be receiving an education.

When I read their answers on scraps of lined paper, I squinted my eyes to make sense of the words. Some of them wrote in really large handwriting, which was helpful to me, but probably would have burned the eyes of another professor. Others wrote in cursive, which I didn't understand the need for, but remembered that primary school education here involves forcing the students to connect letters and seal their edges shut. Cursive exacerbated my blurry vision but I was still able to read the gist of it.

o

Some of the notes are in my file, over there, the last shelf to your right. There's a whole lot of papers in there, but be careful with opening the file. I don't want to lose any of them.

Yasmeen walks over to the shelf and picks up a large black two-holed binder. Growing bulkier per year, it has morphed into a shrine of letters, notes, classroom assignments that I loved, and scraps of poetry that my students had written over the years. I ask her to hand it over as I hold my memories closely like a mother holds her firstborn, not sure whether she loves the baby now outside her womb, or the memory of her baby kicking her stomach for the first time. I touch each paper carefully, afraid it will lose more of its already faded ink. We start looking at them and I tell her to flip to the very end, because that's where the first pages are from this part of the narrative. Some of the students have written:

"I want to be here 'cause my mom did not go to uni and I want my daughter and mom to know I did my best." And another: "English is soo hard but I want to be a English teacher," and "I want to pass this class, I took it before so many times but now I must pass."

These were just a couple of the answers and I started thinking about how these young women reacted to Desdemona's character in the play. Once introduced to Shakespearean drama, they were mortified with how similar Desdemona's fate was to theirs. Desdemona had committed an unutterable crime of choosing to marry against her father's (Brabantio) wishes. Desdemona falls in love with Othello, the Moor, someone of a different race, different social class, and with slavery in his ancestral background. In Renaissance ideology and culture, there is no way that East and West ever meet. A hierarchical society was the basis of all interactions between people and Shakespeare best exemplifies this in his characters' transgressive behaviour. All star-crossed lovers must bear the burden of society's exclusion of them and even desire to ruin their happy union. I explained the term "hierarchy" by slowly pronouncing it to the class, facing them, asking them to repeat the syllables after me. I was relieved the word didn't have an "s" in it and I wouldn't have to embarrass myself as I slurred my syllables.

After the students seemed to have seized the word by the throat, I heard the stress on the letter "r" as though they were suppressing their anger. I reached over to the marker and headed to the whiteboard to draw what a hierarchal society could look like.

"Ah, I remember this exercise really well. You always

used to do it when explaining difficult terms. I didn't think it goes that far back and includes Shakespearean classes. I thought it was just for theory class," Yasmeen says, bringing us back to the present moment.

I look at her and then close my eyes, leaning against the pillow that was helping me sit up on my blue couch, the one I had bought with my first paycheck. Closing my eyes, I can see the blue and red ink on the whiteboard, two markers used to separate gender, class, and disability.

o

I remember the feel of the marker as I pressed hard to make sure the students could see. As if tormenting my anxieties, a student immediately piped up, "We can't see!"

You'd think it was the marker's fault. But it was mine, I couldn't tell if I had pushed hard enough, and my blurry vision couldn't tell if I was the only one able to see the words or the students huddled in the back could see. Silently, I pressed harder, going over the initial lettering, hoping twice written would suffice. The students sitting in the front row observed my moves and tilted their heads in curiosity. My cane fell on the ground as I had lost my balance, and one student rushed forward to catch it. She leaned over and handed it to me as I mouthed my thank-you. As she stood before me, I asked her to stay and finish my ladder of hierarchy. I took a seat and looked at her, all excited, ready to go.

"What's your name?" I asked, playing with my cane to lighten the mood.

"Badriya," she answered excitedly, pen pointing at the whiteboard, ready to be thrown like a dart.

"Great, Badriya, I want you to help us map the world. If the world was a hierarchy, a social ladder of who has more rights, who is more respected, what would it look like? Your colleagues will help." I turned to face the class. "We have to see this clearly and I am sure you all have different ways of looking. There isn't one way to draw this, so if you feel otherwise, just add branches to your map. Let me start with the first. Who usually has the most power, in *Othello*, in societies, and even today? White, upper-class, rich, healthy, hetero-sexual men."

"Well, Professor, here people aren't white. But they're still powerful men. It depends on their family name, their tribe, their social class," one young woman, Monira, interjected. She was right, and I was thrilled to see how quickly she had picked up.

We went on to outline the way the social ladder puts men on top, regardless of class, disability, and income. The women argued that even a disabled man would have a higher chance of leading a productive life, while a disabled woman would come next in line, having lost the ability to be considered equal to other healthy women. The ladder kept growing and when Badriya made the final marks, they all sat there, dumb-founded, frustrated, and repeating the words "not fair." Women came in last, women with lower socio-economic status, no citizenship, disabilities, a woman who is not the wife of someone; a single, citizen-less woman with a disability hung on to the bottom of the ladder, the last step in Badriya's visualisation.

"That's why education is important. You can't do anything without education," one of the older women commented. She was sitting in the front of the class-room and peered at me from behind her framed glasses.

"Yeah, but you can have a degree and not have a passport, and good luck finding a job!" responded one of the younger women.

"I raised three boys on my own, their father was an alcoholic and abusive. I ran away with my boys. I worked sewing people's clothes for many years until I made sure all the boys went to university. Now it's my turn to get an education, so they can be proud of their Mama," the older woman stated calmly.

"They should be proud of you anyway," the younger woman replied.

"Ah, you young people think everything is something to be proud of. Not everything is a badge you can wear and say 'look, look at what I can do!' We just did what we had to do. Not something to be proud of. Mothers raise children and Allah never leaves us behind. I just did what I had to do, for them, and now this is for me. So, Desdemona is smart for choosing to do what she wanted for herself."

I smiled at the conversation inspired by the term "hierarchy" and began to circle back to the play. I asked the older woman for her name and she replied that her name was Sukayna. Sukayna was happy to read Desdemona's lines out while I helped her with her pronunciation. Her voice boomed across the classroom for the rest of that semester, always embodying the full character of Desdemona.

Midway through that semester, Othello loses his mind. He believes the play's villain, Iago, and is utterly convinced that his wife is cheating on him. In comes the play's greatest questions, ones that literary critics have asked repeatedly, and these same questions always heat up a classroom discussion. There is always so much to say when we think about the major question: who is to blame for Othello's tragedy? He kills his wife because he is convinced that she has "cuck-olded" him, to use the Renaissance term, and later kills himself in a tragic ending to the love story. Many critics believe it is Iago's evil manipulation of Othello that drives the play's hero to his destruc-tion. Others believe it is, in fact, Othello's own doing and undoing of his life that causes the tragic ending. Othello's insecurity drives him to believe Iago's insin-uations and makes him an easy target, a sponge ready to soak up Iago's evil plan to destroy Othello and Desdemona.

This brings us to one of the most significant ideas in literature, stretching as far back to Greek tragedy and Aristotle's definition of the tragic flaw, which he refers to as "hamartia." The tragic flaw is the one flaw that leads to the protagonist's demise. Usually, it is an inter-nal flaw, one that is motivated and nourished by one's own ego, insecurity, and leads to an error of judge-ment. I take the idea of the tragic flaw to mean errors that could in fact be avoided if the hero of the play was able to look outside of themselves to see beyond their own bubble. Some of my students, especially the women, looked at Othello as a villain, a murderer who deserves his tragic fortune of losing the love of his life and later on takes his own life, too. They were angered that Othello did not appreciate Desdemona's initial fight for their love. Others sympathised with Othello and believed that it was society's fault that he had become so deranged and insecure.

"If you think about it, most lovers are just not logical. They're crazy," Maha said, one of my quieter students.

"Doesn't excuse it. You know we put up with so much just because we always try to excuse things as women. Why should we excuse Othello, too?" Fatima replied, sitting in the back, looking up from her phone and glaring at Maha's back.

"I think we all try so hard to make sense of men's behaviour and society's behaviour, but really, it's important to be an adult about things. Othello is just a big man-child," Badriya added. "What do your male students think, Professor? We never get to hear their thoughts."

The men's class was reacting differently to the play. None of them had sided with Desdemona, at least not vocally. During class discussions, I would read Desdemona's lines and have the men read the rest of the characters' lines. When we got to the final scene where Othello is debating whether to kill Desdemona or not, one of the students, Ahmad, scratched his head as he read Othello's lines to us:

> *It is the cause, it is the cause, my soul.*
> *Let me not name it to you, you chaste stars,*
> *It is the cause. Yet I'll not shed her blood,*
> *Nor scar that whiter skin of hers than snow*
> *And smooth as monumental alabaster.*
> *Yet she must die, else she'll betray more men.*
> *Put out the light, and then put out the light.*
> *(Act 5, scene 2)*

We paused and took in the words. Ahmad looked at me for a reaction and the other students had their pens ready to dissect the text. Annotation is never the only part of teaching a complex literary text. I always let the reader breathe through the anxiety of the text. Foreign languages (like English for my students) needed to be approached gently. We work through the apprehension together. Jokingly, I would provide multiple choice definitions in Arabic so that they could find the meaning in context. So, I asked about the repetition of the word "cause" and what it could mean. Othello provides a cause, lifts his arms to the stars and sky, wanting guidance for his dilemma. His conflict is obvious to the audience, but was it clear to my students?

"Why does Othello feel so torn apart?" I asked, searching their faces for answers. Many of them had lightened up and looked at me more freely. Some of them would still not look me in the eye, seeing me as a female teacher who they preferred not to look at, whether because of religious reasons or tribal beliefs. Once, I overheard one of them saying, "She comes from a tribe that is powerful. My family knows all of her uncles." I pretended not to hear the comment and continued on, briefcase in hand.

"Professor, he loves her. Love is blind, they say. He needs to do the right thing," Sulaiman, one of the more outspoken ones, answered. "He has to kill her and cleanse her soul and his name."

It was difficult for me to remain composed while I felt the feminist in me battle against the misogyny. I knew my students didn't have the vocabulary to locate or label misogyny. I asked them to vote instead. How many thought Othello had to kill Desdemona, in agreement with Sulaiman? Every hand shot up, except for two, one who eventually raised his hand reluctantly. Looking at them with their arms above their heads made me lean against my cane for balance.

"You're kidding me! What hope do we have if that was the vote?" Yasmeen huffs angrily. She gets up to grab a bottle of lemonade from my fridge and asks me if I want one, too.

It was precisely that question that I carried with me. I wondered if I was capable of causing any change at all, if this was the reaction that I had received from them. Misogyny was alive and well. What could I possibly do to sway them just a little? I wanted to talk about love, because I had grown up understanding that you can only fight hatred with love, that you can only liberate and heal with love. I wasn't one to carry a sword around or even a protest sign (although as you know I admire and respect those who are able to), so I resorted to the language Mama had taught me.

But if Othello fought for Desdemona, and loves her faithfully as he says, why is he so quickly tempted to let that love go? If love is the driving force behind Othello's actions, what kills the love? Is it him? Is it society? Is it Iago? I prompted them with so many questions and stared intently at their faces as their brows tightened and they shifted uncomfortably in their seats, glancing at each other for support. I was outnumbered, and yet they were obviously unhappy with my probing at a long-buried body.

When one of the young men started talking, the rest joined. I don't remember who started the conversation, but the word "aib" kept popping up, thrown in like a filler, a stop to all conversations. It was the word that meant culturally inappropriate, taboo, shameful. It was aib for Othello to let Desdemona cheat on him and not wash his shame and hers away. What would people say? His reputation was stained forever. Better a murderer than a shamed man. What man? What is a real man if he can't wash his shame? Aib, Professor. Aib.

They agreed that Othello was struggling because he was a victim. Society had killed his love for Desdemona and later forced him to kill himself, too. There would be no other way out, but death. In other words, society had won, and individual love was too mediocre. After nearly forty minutes of class discussion, I asked them to consider how hard life was for Othello and to imagine what life would be like for Desdemona. Or a woman. A woman whose fate was in the hands of men, all the time. Their faces went dark and some began to shake their heads.

"This is too sad. So much drama," one of them said.

"It is drama. Who says life isn't one big drama?" I asked.

"But it's too much. Women can even vote now. They're not like Desdemona."

"Yes, but how many of your sisters would defy the tribe? The family? How many would have a voice of their own?"

"It's different, Professor. This is a story. Our lives are not a story."

I can't say we got anywhere. But if you're looking for the silver lining, on one of the days, at the end of the semester, when we were saying our goodbyes and had finished *Othello* and *The Duchess of Malfi* and the killing of women in Renaissance culture, the young men thanked me and left the class with smiles. And then two of them stayed behind. One of them said he had something to say, while the other fiddled with his phone, waiting for Nawaf to finish his speech.

"I just want to say that we are very proud of you, Professor. You are a woman, but you are trying so hard. It's even hard for you to walk and stand, but you always gave us everything you could. I want my sisters to be like you. May Allah bless you," Nawaf said, his hand above his crown, a gesture of respect. "Ala rasi Diktorah."

I returned the gesture by placing my hand above my heart, and Nawaf left the classroom for the last time and waved goodbye at me. I looked at the only student left, Abdulaziz, and asked him how I could help. He replied by asking me to wait in the classroom while he went to get something. I nodded and agreed to wait. Only a few minutes later, a woman walked in with him. She walked behind him, extremely shy and hesitant to approach me. I smiled, anticipating an introduction. Abdulaziz introduced her as "my wife, Om Faisal." He beamed at me and she extended her hand warmly and then asked if she could hug me. I leaned in.

She had wanted to meet me to thank me for being an inspiration to her husband and helping her deal with him. She explained he had changed so much since taking the class with me, and she was grateful. I don't know how he had changed and I don't know the dynamic of their relationship, but I remember that image very well: him, blushing, and her, repeating her thank-yous excitedly. Abdulaziz responded to her accusation "he never listens to me" by saying, "It's easier to listen to the professor talk about women." She laughed and said, "That's why I had to thank you. Our marriage became stronger because we were always talking about Othello and Desdemona. You made him see what's it like to be a wife."

Each one of my students had a story. One of my students, Janna, would always bring her two children with her to class. One was a seven-year-old boy, and the other was a five-year-old girl. I wish I could say I remember their names. But the boy would sit in the front row, and the girl would sit in her lap throughout the class. He was too short for the chairs and his legs would dangle, his straight long hair falling into his eyes as he hummed to himself while I rambled on with big words. Sometimes, I would stop in the middle of the lecture and ask him how he was doing, or if I bored him. He would nod and affirm my suspicions.

"Yalla, soon you get to go home," I would say with a

wink. Janna explained to me that her husband allowed her to come to classes only if the children were with her. Most professors would agree to having the children join her, while others would insist that they stay seated outside, her heart with them all the time, her mind on student-mode. She asked me if I had any advice for her as she struggled to get her professors to listen to her circumstances. Some would firmly refuse and tell her that an education wasn't for everyone. Being a mother meant being a mother, and that was the path she had chosen, they would lecture. Janna's eyes were always so wide, and her tone was always so exasperated. She wanted badly to understand why academics weren't more understanding and why there were so many guarding the magical door of education. Her husband wouldn't budge, and neither would her professors, and she had to bridge the gap between her desires and her limitations. She was also working a morning shift as a receptionist while her children were in school so that she could afford her tuition fees. Her mother would try her best to help her on days where she wasn't allowed to bring her children to class, or days where she would have an exam and need to be focused solely on taking it. Janna always finished her exams early, rushing to leave campus, always in a hurry to get back to her motherly duties. Her name, Janna, which meant "Heaven," prompted me to remind her we are told "al-janna tahta aqdam al-omahat." She would always pause to take a breath and beam at me after listening to this sentence, which I thought was so cliché, but to her, meant the world. Janna graduated, went on to raise her children, and became a teacher herself.

o

"I think you gave all of these people a sense of belong-ing, at least in class," Yasmeen says, scratching Lucky's head.

Perhaps what I wanted more than anything at the time was to find meaning in teaching, meaning in my life, and to help somehow. I still run into some of my students from time to time and forget their names, but always return the "salam." The first time I got stopped while buying my groceries I heard the word "Diktorah" and turned around and found a smiling face of a man I didn't recognise. Days and months change people and years make them unrecognisable to me. But the feeling? The feeling of being recognised and held in a student's memory keeps me alive. Even when I cannot recognise the faces anymore, love blooms in my chest as I am grateful to still be alive. To see and be seen.

Chapter O of Four

Diary Entry: "When we fail at being who we are supposed to be, does that mean we can still find love? I am searching for answers and I think I have found one. When we fail, we have to hold each other up and bring love to the table. When I can't feed myself self-love, my circle does that for me. Circles are an act of hope, a continuation, an overflow."

Yasmeen has managed to pick out diary entries over the years and read them according to themes she felt she needed to talk about with me. We had always debated the big things in class, and now we were looking at abstract ideas, picked from my diary, like dead roses meant for potpourri. She had flipped through the pages and prompted me with each entry, and I found myself thinking about how thoughts change with time. The one constant is change, Mama used to say, and I know this is yet another one of her unquoted lines of wisdom. Change is part of who we are and our lives hit different climactic and anticlimactic phases. But like a circle, we keep going, and it becomes harder to find the beginning, middle, and end, and even more difficult to locate a climax.

Mama would always draw circles, and I would watch the rhythm of her hands as they continued. Circles, never rigid, flexible, willing to bend but not be bent, not be broken. Mama would ask me to study the circle and consider its wholeness, its unity.

Circles are also protective and embracing. Think of every time we used to sit in a circle in class. Think of that all-inclusive space, the space of oneness, where teacher and student meet, where you get to look at your colleagues, your eyes meet, and there are no spaces crowded with desks separating you. Circles and spheres are all around in divine symbols, think of the planets, the sun, the growth rings in trees, raindrops, and even our cells. They are tied to movement and stillness holding you in, keeping you safe as the centre holds you.

As someone living with chronic illness, there are many limitations to what constitutes a good and happy life. Nothing fits in boxes anymore and I cannot look at life as one straight, narrow arrow. Illness has had a circular effect. The clock ticks, the day ends and repeats itself, the doctors' visits become repetitive, and I come back full circle to a damaged central nervous system. The result is the same, but that doesn't mean the path ever stops. We create new meanings using the self-stories we tell about ourselves, too. Each new story leads to another story, each thought adds to our self-perception, and as we add more thoughts, the cycle of life continues. Our psyche feeds on these self-stories and we can look at the world softly. I feel safer within a circle and I look at life and my illness as perfect circles, the ultimate geometric shape, a shape that has meaning even in its seemingly meaningless recurrences.

When illness enters the picture, life has to take a different course. Every day with MS is random, and this randomness is not easy to accept. The narrative of illness can feel circular, oscillating between periods of health and cycles of debilitation, and at other times continuously debilitating until the end of life. I know I would like to stay on the Ferris wheel, as scary as it is, as apprehensive as I feel about it at times. I have wanted to end my life due to the physical pain and have thought there is no way out. I have considered different end-of-life regimes and thought about whether euthanasia is an option. I have been dangerously sad and at other times dangerously persistent to keep going, to stay on the wheel of life. I have held on tightly to stories and to creating new definitions of selfhood, new self-stories that would hold me in place as the safety belt began to fray. Each time I lost a sense (like my hearing, my vision), even if temporarily, it was hard to keep loving myself. It was harder to keep seeing pain as having an end. I am thinking of Emily Dickinson's poem "Pain has an element of blank." When I used to teach this poem of hers, I used to envision the circle again.

"I always thought the poem was about heartbreak and loss," Yasmeen comments.

Heartbreak and loss are connected, again, to our self-stories. Our ideas of whether we deserve to be loved or deserve to soak up the pain. Dickinson's poem reminds us that pain can become a state of being suspended in time, not knowing where you are, when the pain will stop. But even in that dark hole there is some sort of circulating back to the same pain, that it becomes normalised. There is an awakening, a moment where we understand the chaos, and know that there will be new pain. Not all people who live with pain are engulfed in darkness or can only see the darkness. Many disabled people are, in fact, quite happy individuals, unlike the myth that society feeds us. We even look at a disabled or ill person and say "Alhamdillah wa ilshukur" to thank God for blessing us with health, further alienating disabled individuals. I saw clearer when I noticed that the circle is part of the narrative, its temporalities and inconsistencies bringing me closer to myself and others. I began not only to speak, but also to listen more.

○

I listened to my students living with cancer, chronic illnesses, and disabilities. At the beginning of every class, I would read the disability accommodation statement and ask them to share their needs with me so that I could accommodate and make sure the classroom was accessible. We didn't have all of the accessibility needed in terms of university architecture, buildings, classroom spaces, and even textbooks were not always available in Braille or as audiobooks. Lack of access was part of societal barriers to disabled individuals' success. It was not the disability itself. My blind students and I were able to connect and discuss how disability is treated in our Arab society and what obstacles are constantly faced by them. I asked if "visually impaired" was a better term and two of them agreed that the term "blind" was more honest. People tiptoe around the term just like they tiptoe around their blindness. Disability exists, there is no need to sugarcoat it.

One of them, Wajd, had asserted that she hated how people never spoke directly to her. They would speak to the helper who would assist her on her way to classes and would ignore Wajd's presence.

"It's like they can't see me, Professor! It's like they're the blind ones!" she exclaimed, frustrated with the lack of awareness. "I don't understand why sight is about seeing instead of about basic courtesy. They should see me for who I am," she went on.

Wajd was one of my brightest students, and I learned how to be more conscious of my speech patterns while having her in my classes throughout the years. I would always end my classes with a casual "see you tomorrow" until she pointed out there would be no "seeing." I switched to "meet you all tomorrow" and it stuck with me as my new catchphrase. Every time my tongue slipped, I circled back to her voice in my head, that year that I taught her. We shared thoughts about disability and exchanged notes on what it was like to be a disabled woman, seen for being disabled, but unseen as a woman.

"We have to work twice as hard to prove ourselves. We try to make people see us all the time. I want what every girl wants, and even more. I'm not that Blind Girl. I am the girl who wants to be a Professor," Wajd would say.

My other student who was blind, Ali, had a different perspective because of his gender, of course. He insisted that women romanticised him too much.

"It's like that movie with Al Pacino, that really old movie."

"*Scent of a Woman*? I love that movie," I said.

"Yeah, but Professor, not every blind guy is going to be hopelessly romantic and woo every girl he talks to. I want to be seen as just a guy. I want them to be mad at me sometimes, too. I don't want to always be seen as Mr. Nice Guy, harmless 'cause he's blind," Ali explained. It didn't help that he played the piano, too, and was really great at it. Magical hands, I teased him.

"Yeah, but see, that's the image the girls see. Magical and all, but not the type you'd marry. I am tired of girls wanting to take care of me. I'm not a child."

I thought of what Ali had said and what Wajd had said and explained to both of them (on separate occasions) that ableism was not always so clear. That it occurs in the smaller instances, microaggressions that aren't always easy to spot. Microaggressions make you feel bad, you feel a small raging fire start in your chest, and it grows until you can't remember how it all started. Microaggressions can be verbal and non-verbal, environmental, slurs, or societal. They can be there in front of you, reachable, or they can be dust particles invisible to the naked eye—the eye that is non-disabled, the eye that has been sheltered for so long, non-naked in every respect. Disabled people can pick up on these everyday nuances and yet struggle to explain why it is a problem when the majority don't encounter the same problem. It becomes your problem as the minority, your problem for being disabled, your problem for being too sensitive.

Ali explained to me that his male friends considered him lucky because he could talk to girls. He was an excellent conversationalist and spent a lot of his time understanding people. He would read all about emotional intelligence and learned to read social cues from the way people spoke and changed their tones. It was important for him to listen more, to listen really hard, put in double the effort for a conversation to go smoothly. And most guys didn't do that, he stated, matter-of-factly.

"It seems all the disabled people you mentioned put in double the work." Yasmeen continues, "I feel strange about that. I feel sorry for them, not because of the disability, but because they have to try so hard."

It's easy to fall into the trap of pitying disabled people. It's also easy to be completely inspired by us. There seem to be two opposing reactions to disability. Pity, fear, and disgust, or on the opposite end of the spectrum, inspiration, awe, and excessive admiration.

In all cases, the disability is what is seen, not the person. The person is reduced to the disability and how they manage or don't manage it. I have heard the sentence "you're so inspiring" thousands of times and each time I take a step back and wonder if I would be as inspiring without my disability featuring as a huge part of my life.

I remember teaching R.J. Palacio's children's novel *Wonder* and discussing the protagonist Auggie's facial defect as part of his experience being bullied and othered in school. Some students at the time found him to be an inspiring character, while at the same time wondering if including Auggie in school with other "normal" children was the right thing to do. Integrating Auggie with able-bodied children sounded very harsh to them, a decision that they weren't sure they would actually make if their child was disabled. Teaching the novel brought so many questions to the forefront. I could see the difference between able-bodied attitudes and disabled attitudes, while trying to bridge the gap between the two. Some of my students were also mothers, and they felt that being a mother meant protecting your child from being bullied, that there was no need to expose the disabled individual to the cruelty of the world.

I went home to my mother with this information and placed it in front of her. I told her that the students felt that cruelty would be allowing the child to have a normal life. She was fuming by the time I finished relaying the information.

"Cruel mothers? They're still mothers. They want what's best for you. Why should we stop the child from growing up and falling and getting hurt? Why should we control the environment that they're in? Either way, we all die. Mothers will go. The shield will disintegrate and you will find that the child has to survive. The mother can be the cane to lean on in the early years, but at some point, the child will have their prosthetic leg. That may not be a 'normal' leg, but it will do. I don't understand why people think a disabled child will never grow up. They look at disabled adults as children, too. It bothers me, but all I can say is we aren't doing any favours by protecting our children. Society is the problem, and you better keep teaching your students, keep trying. Push the door open just a bit, and see who walks through the door," Mama said. She paused for a long time and then finally added, "It's a circle. You give others and they will give others. Pass it on. Pass the candle and let it light someone's path."

Mothering is a complicated state of being, and one that I don't have experience in. I have heard my good friends describe it as a state of having your heart walk around and knowing it will get shattered at any second. I am thinking of my circle of friends, friends who are mothers, friends who aren't mothers but who hold each other up. A circle of women who support women. My friends have been my support system, and I have been theirs. My disability has always featured as part of all of my connections to others, and certainly it has affected my closest relationships. All of my good friends are able-bodied and have had their youth's narrative unaffected by illness or a sudden disability. They have struggled to understand my body's faltering and limitations. Only one of my friends, Farida, a mother raising her autistic child, Dana, has come so close to the experience of living with a disability in an ableist and exclusionary society.

Farida, being a mother herself, had understood that disability was not only tied to the body, but to society's cruelty. Her daughter had grown up with only Farida's support and I had watched her carefully, observing the amount of love and friendship that Farida offered her daughter. And she did it all on her own. I was there as a good friend, lending an ear, a space to crash on my couch, to vent, to play video games with Dana, to ensure that she knew she wasn't alone. I loved Dana very much and felt as though I understood her sensory difficulties, her hatred for loud noises, her agitation with flashing lights on a television screen, and her neurodivergence. Many years ago, I listened to Farida rage against Dana's father and his lack of understanding of his daughter's neurodivergence and his refusal to accept the diagnosis. I asked her to write about it. At first, she was hesitant, thinking that nobody would want to read about her rage, her frustration, and that this narrative was too personal, too different from others' experiences. But I insisted that her experience as a mother, as a caregiver, was an experience that was much needed. Dana would grow up knowing her mother's experience was as valid as hers. Caregiver experiences tend to be either too emphasised or too decentralised.

o

I want to include pieces of Farida's account which she published years ago, pull it up from the binder.

Yasmeen hands me the binder and I pull the heaviness of memory lane into my lap. There is a beautiful familiarity in the pages and each paper I flip through feels as though I am leafing through an archive of memories. I had stored these pages and now was retrieving them to guide myself out of the isolation I had been feeling. With my MS progressing, I was feeling more isolated than ever. I had begun to turn inwards and could hardly remember how my circle of friends and connections had always kept me going. I was searching for guidance and I wanted to read Farida's words again, share them with Yasmeen, use their maternal power to heal. The words are meant to be read out loud, to be used to console us and give a voice to the experience of being Farida, a mother, a friend, part of my circle of survival.

The letters are not blurry. The words are clear but my eyelids are heavy. I squint at them and wear my eyeglasses, thinking that will solve the issue. But I know better. I ask Yasmeen to read the article, handing the paper to her, almost as if lending her my voice and Farida's, a generation to speak with the other, an able-bodied woman speaking with (not for) the disabled community. I want the experience to be visceral for her as she reads the words out loud. Just like my experience teaching poetry, telling my students to read the words out loud, hear the rhythm rise and stretch, bring meaning to the poet's experience. We all suffer differently, but each suffering has a rhythm, a quality that is to be recognised in its difference. I don't want to lose sight of suffering as part of our circle, part of the reason we connect so strongly, our similarities as women, whether able-bodied or disabled, and yet I need to emphasise the differences. But the differences are meant to be a bridge that connects, rather than separates. We have a bridge between us, and we access it willingly because we built it together over the years.

Farida and I still live next door to each other and our experiences with disability became part of the communal energy that we put in our everyday lives. Each meal she cooked for her daughter, she would send half of it to me. Each time I got some groceries I would send some over to her. We had, as the Egyptians say, aish wa milh shared between us. Bread and salt, bread and butter, bread and anything you want it to be, but this act of sharing food was a part of the bridge that helped us stay afloat. Above water. Always, together, knowing that family was a women's circle that wanted to ensure you stayed alive. There have been many times where I would not leave my bed but would have to get up because Farida and Dana were knocking at the door, a hot meal in hand, and would burst through my apartment, opening the windows, making my home their home.

Farida had felt abandoned by Dana's father, and I knew what that was like too well. Farida had dedicated her entire life to raising Dana and being her father and mother, her best friend, and her support system. Because the law discriminated against women who remarried (and would give custody of their children to the ex-husband), Farida refused to get to know anyone who could possibly fall in love with her. She constantly turned down potential suitors and struggled to make sense of her feelings. Sometimes she would feel a spark, a connection, and then completely shut it off. She would come to me and explain that her life was no longer hers, and that it was all Dana's. She wouldn't lose her, no matter how much she had her own desires for another marriage and a life companion. The law was unfair, but it was the law. The law wouldn't make room for specifics. The law didn't understand human emotion and the intricacies of desire. You fall in love; you lose custody of your children. You are deemed unfit to be a mother? You lose custody. If they don't go to their father, then they go to your mother, or your sister, but not you. And Farida wouldn't allow the law to dictate where her daughter would live and who would love her the most.

"That's a good mother," Yasmeen says, reaching over to read the words. "But it's really all about sacrifice."

"I think she really didn't look at it as a sacrifice. It was all from a place of love. She became so good at it. She wasn't born a natural mother. I don't think anyone ever is. The more she learned about mothering Dana and finding the right balance between letting her grow up into being her own person and suffocating her, the more she learned about love. Love meant being in the circle but allowing Dana to leave the circle and come back at her own will. Read the words out loud, I love listening to their beat, the tension between falling apart and trying to fight for her daughter when everyone else gave up on her."

Yasmeen starts reading out loud and each word transports me to Farida's voice:

> *At the age of 1.3 years, my daughter was diagnosed with autism spectrum disorder. My husband at the time did not believe it. He thought the diagnosis would wreck our daughter's future, and if we "ignored the label" she would be better off. My husband refused to participate in anything related to her well-being or even daily routine. Which just prepped me and gave me more time to practice being the single mum I currently am. The autism diagnosis didn't break my marriage, ignorance did. All those nights of me listening to the negative comments of how my daughter can never be "normal" and "isn't acting like children her age" strengthened me and made me more determined to focus on her, and only her. I devoted all my free time to being the only caregiver and to support her in every possible way. Loving her and being loved by her has been my miracle. ("The Mighty")*

As Dana grew up, she constructed more sentences and developed friendships with her peers and her mother's circle of friends. We all felt responsible for her and the love grew in the circle as birthdays, Ramadan, Eid, and every holiday was shared. It was a circle of trust and friendship, and I think back now and cannot imagine what my life would have been like without my circle.

There are many disabilities and all sorts of ways that we experience our minds and bodies. Mama still paints on a canvas and allows me to watch the colours melt into each other. I ask her why the colours aren't part of a plan, and how she knows when the painting is finished. She always says that the colours are their own people, they are their own agents; they decide where to go, which path to take, where they will end up. She would pour the paint and watch it take a different shape every few minutes. We would stand above the painting, watching the paint pluralise, part ways, pair itself with other colours. And the painting is never really finished, you just decide to get up when it feels like an ending. It doesn't mean that it's a real ending, because who's to say you can't go back and change it? Each colour is unique, but it can also give you a new shade once it blends with another colour. And it's hard to find the same shade again, the exact hues. They're all colours but will function differently on every canvas.

o

We all react differently to the sudden onset of illness, while others are born with a disability and that has always been the life that they have known. Others live a good life and then have a tragic event shatter them one day. Like Lara. Lara, one of my best friends. Lara, who was always the adventurous and daring one.

Lara's experience with illness was different. She had started her life as a sports fanatic, someone who was so healthy and built so strong, so sturdy. Lara was the person I could turn to (and Farida could, too) for advice about pain, heartbreak, and how to live without a man in a society that expects you to be successfully married, someone's happy (and healthy) wife. Lara was passionate, loving, and most of all, had always loved too hard. Lara had married, early in her life, the man who she believed was the love of her life. They travelled the world together and brought back memories from each place they visited and hung them on the refrigerator. They had it all—it seemed. Amr was her person, her choice, and she had been his. Until an unexpected visitor showed up.

Doctors diagnosed Lara with severe endometriosis. She could not remain the lively and active person she had been, and was constantly living with pain. Pain changed the person she was, and she started hating her body. Amr was frustrated, she became a shadow of her former self: depressed, unwilling to socialise, to travel, and the pain swallowed her whole. After trying many types of hormone therapy, having her uterus removed was the only option left. She and Amr fought about it for two years before she could no longer stand the pain. She had the hysterectomy done, and he felt betrayed, more than ever before. He didn't even drive her home that day. I did. I heard her cry next to me and remained silent, unsure of what to say, knowing fully well that sometimes language doesn't stop the bleeding. It was her turn to grieve her body and her crumbled marriage. There would be no consolation for that, coming from me. Someone who hadn't understood the promises they had made to each other, the vows they had given, and couldn't imagine her loss. But I understood living with chronic pain was a journey with no end. And having her uterus removed was part of the end to pain, but a start to an unfamiliar pain and she would be called to re-imagine herself and a new life without Amr. There would be no children of her own, like she had always wanted. They had always dreamed of having two children, a girl and a boy, but put it off until they travelled most of the world on their own. Freedom-loving as they were, Lara and Amr could not imagine being constrained, constricted to anything, and when pain tied Lara's body to a couch, he struggled to see her.

Lara had to envision a new life for herself and needed to be around her friends, but not before a year of therapy, a year of trying to label her despair, and finding it hard to fashion a new identity. Who was she now? She struggled to find love again—and when she finally did, the men she met would leave after finding out she could not have the babies they wanted. Adoption was not a topic they were interested in, many of them insisting that a baby had to look like them, have their genes, and there would be no negotiations. I still think she will adopt a child on her own, because she has always loved too hard. She has a lot of love to give. She struggled to turn that love inwards when she felt that her body had betrayed her. But we all waited for her. We waited until she moved into a new apartment, changed her job, started going for morning walks. We waited until she started joining our gatherings again. We waited until she started laughing again. Lara came back up, gasping for air, and found her friends waiting for her.

But there are others who don't have friends waiting

for them. There was Dahlia, Lara's sister-in-law. I had known Dahlia for a couple of years, when she was in her late forties. She was a psychologist who fell into a severe depression after her husband cheated on her. Her depression quickly turned into a volcano that erupted inside of her. She divorced him to start a new life and heal. After freeing herself from him, she lost everyone that loved her. Her family and friends stopped talking to her. She was now die-vorced. Dead to them. The shame of her second divorce was too much to bear. Dahlia first divorced at the age of twenty, and then had continued her life after that first failed marriage. She became a doctor and her family were proud of her for cancelling out the negative points of a failed marriage by her newfound status as psychologist. She moved on from the first failure into the arms of a narcissist who gaslighted her constantly.

She would find remains of lipstick on his white collar, and he would yell at her for doubting him. He would constantly call her "crazy" and label her as obsessive, possessive, insecure. All sorts of words. Dahlia could not tell me her story until she was free of him. He had tried to sabotage her career by sending emails to her colleagues and letting them know she was going through a difficult time and was not functioning at her best. Dahlia's colleagues believed him, because he was an established general surgeon— he was trustworthy. She lost most of the people who believed in her and eventually lost faith in herself. Dahlia's depression consumed her. She struggled to reach out to others and couldn't bear the idea of being sick. What eventually saved Dahlia was a complete life-makeover. She changed her career, enrolled in various body healing courses, and a spiritual path opened up for her. She followed that path and became an energy healer herself, reaching out to others and offering her support through a path that blended science with spirituality. She found her circle of healers and a community that believed in love regardless of social class and what job you held. They simply wanted to spread love and make others feel like they could belong.

What I have always found profoundly interesting is the way people create their own circles and this circle becomes the element of healing, giving, and receiving. It is a circle of love and extends to others. When people take their suffering and pain and mesh it with others' colours, you get a different colour to the pain.

o

"There's an excerpt here and you've titled it 'Circles and Dance,'" Yasmeen interjects.

Yes, I wrote it for a beautiful disability journal. The journal was great because they wanted to hear about disabled writers' experiences. I was thinking of how life becomes more vibrant by us witnessing each other's lives, by listening, by leaning in closer, by staying. When we witness each other's lives, it reminds us that we are really truly here.

> *Perhaps I resisted the urge to ask you to stay for too long. I wanted to retain my autonomy and remind myself and you that I would not be dependent on you. That I wouldn't need to lean on you during those long strolls we take across the city, admiring the skyscrapers, while I start feeling my feet lose their direction. I wanted to know that I was still attractive as I fumbled across the room to get to you. One, two steps, and the third was the fall. The first time I fell down I felt the shame surge and enter the room challenging one of*

*us to respond, to leave, to exit stage. And yet again
you stayed.*

*Coordination became even more difficult, and
connecting my brain cells to my right foot and right
hand was maddening. The information teleported by
my nerves would stop half-way through and I would
freeze and panic, unable to remember which limb
was being spoken to. I would pause and stare at the
floor. And then you took my hand and started dancing
with me. Dance helped me to reconnect to my body
and infused my nerves with a new second-language.
Two steps. One, two. Here we go. One, two. Movement together. ("Staying and Witnessing: Two Steps
of Love")*

Chapter U of Four

Diary Entry: "Tell all the truth—," in line with Emily Dickinson's orders, "but tell it slant—" just say it!

That's all the diary entry says. I want to write a new one. What have I told you so far? I want to circle back to how love brought us here. Stories and literature help us understand trauma. Narrative writing helps to alleviate the pain. As long as the author does not harm the reader, as long as my wounds don't open in a way that will bleed all over the pages and cause a stench of repugnancy. There is always work to be done when we think of storytelling. Even in telling someone else's story, I can never tell it accurately. However, I can empathise, the way we do when we love someone and can imagine what it's like to be them, to put ourselves in their shoes.

"I think even if the story isn't accurate, the heart of the emotion is real. Just listening to you now makes me feel like I've been there, I've felt it all. I still feel like I'm the student, but did you ever feel like you were learning from us?" Yasmeen asks.

o

I remember one of my closest students, challenging my thoughts around safe spaces, home, and when literature can really save us. She was one of my quietest students and seldom had something to say. But Darah stopped me during one of my lectures one day and said, "There's no such thing as a safe space. Anything can stop being safe. There's no home, either. That goes away, too."

I spoke to Darah later and asked her to explain how that could be and what she meant. Darah shrugged her shoulders at me, the way she shrugged her shoulders at everything, her hair falling in her eyes, covering her piercing look. She asked me why I needed an explanation if it was so "obvious." I was a professor of words, wasn't I? I should know better. But I didn't, and I wanted to hear her argument.

"You tell us words are a safe space, and that literature always saves us. You tell us that a home is the safest place you can be. Homes can be safe, but they can also be the worst place you can be. When my mom and dad died, my home was not a home. It wasn't safe, even though I locked the door and made sure my siblings and I stayed inside. Then my aunts came and separated us, took us each into one of their houses. A new home, a new family. There wasn't anything safe about that. I remember my mom used to have the lights on all the time, even if it was early morning. Now the new home doesn't have lights on, ever. I lock my door all the time, because it's not my home."

Darah and I talked for hours that day, in my office, and I went to get us each ice-cream from the vendor next to campus. She was thrilled, and I needed to lighten the mood of our conversation for it to continue. She made me pause and think.

"And literature, Professor, it's fun and all, and it tells stories, but think about how many orphans we read about? Cool orphans, I mean. They're all either really poor and victims, or they're thieves, or they're searching for a new mom. It's not who I am and I can't find myself anywhere," Darah said, staring at her chocolate ice-cream before adding, "I just think literature should include everyone. And if you can write, you need to think about others, too. Like write a story that isn't just yours, but it talks about other people who have a different experience from the majority."

Darah was right. I hadn't thought of the representation of orphans in literature. I had just focused on illness because it concerned me. She had nudged me into expanding my circle and wanting to lend her my voice, too. Darah's vulnerability was a gift she gave me over the years, and she still makes an effort to come and see me and talk to me. Our discussions have always been a privilege, because she looks at me and sees someone who defends storytelling but can listen to her attack storytellers for failing to see. Experiences are vast and the world contains a multitude of stories, but there are only a handful of true storytellers. She was a true storyteller to me, describing how she viewed motherhood as a distant memory, a place that felt like what home "probably felt like," filled with light and hope, almost unreal, the opposite of day-to-day life. She didn't focus on the trauma of loss and death, but insisted that the light she carried with her resulted from her mother's insistence on light being needed even when the sun shone bright.

"You can never have too much sun," Darah would say, always urging me to open the curtains. Every time I reach for the blinds at home, I smile, thinking of her. She urged me to think about definitions we take for granted and allow room for change to come in, for change to be traumatic, healing, part of the narrative. Throughout the years I have known her, I became her friend, her mentor, and she became someone who always reminded me to stay vigilant about listening to others' stories and to not be only concerned with my perception of pain.

o

When Darah and you, Yasmeen, became my friends, I learned a lot from you. Sarah, too. Sarah with her coffee always in hand, her poetry pouring from her lips, sharing her bilingual magic, writing spoken word poetry about grief, pain, love, loss, and mostly instilling hope in others. I watched Sarah turn her poetry into spoken word poetry; I watched her stand onstage and get a crowd yelling for more, and I thought about how she lent her voice to her peers, her friends, to others who couldn't stand onstage. Some were too afraid, others weren't allowed to speak publicly, and others couldn't label their pain. She used her words to speak and took us into her war of words, always challenging us for answers. Sarah sat down in my office many years ago and asked me to write about women's bodies and voices that get silenced. I promised her I would try, when the time was right, when I had something substantial to say. Her response was, "Professor, you're the voice of the universe in my ears. I have it with me all the time. It gets annoying sometimes how right you are, but I still love you!"

And there was Maha, too. Maha who was the first person to read my blog, to know about my MS through reading my work. Maha wrote me a long email one day assuring me that to her, a real professor was someone who would show up for her students no matter what. She became one of my friends after she graduated school and did a program in women's studies in Doha.

I was so proud of her; she was the first in her family to travel abroad. When she received her scholarship, I felt as though I had grown another limb. I smiled when she sent me her schedule of classes, her syllabi, her first academic paper, and when she complained that mental health was still misunderstood in society. Yet she persevered, went to therapy, found ways to stay alive, insisted on going to the gym, on reaching out to her circle of friends. To me, Maha remained one of the limbs I could depend on as a reminder that there was a new generation of women who would challenge the patriarchy. Maha would send me book recommendations, the newest academic titles, conferences, and tried to keep me engaged in the literary world I loved.

The truth is, or as much truth as my words will convey, I brought you only some literary gifts, while all of you gave me multiple gifts that extended beyond the words, beyond the classroom walls, and stretched out into the future. We are given our selves back by giving. My mother always reminded me to give, even if I had little to give, that there would always be a significant return. That Allah would reciprocate the love, but excessively. The trick was to give what you could. Giving builds bridges, a place we can always return to. Now, I lie stretched on my couch, struggling to remember how I ended up here. When I lost Flake, my beautiful golden girl, you reached out to me and I wrote about this bridge between us in one of my articles on loss.

"Yes, I still have a copy of it, and it was a privilege to be included in it," Yasmeen replies, eyes watering as we both see the image flash before us.

The words were long, academic, weary with editing and refashioning, but here are parts of it:

There is healing where I do not expect to find it. There is a gentleness I do not anticipate. I received a message from a former student, telling me she knows I will be okay. She has taken the role of mentor and teacher and I am now the student:

> *Take as much time as you need to find peace and reflect, Professor. Something you taught me how to do. You always tell us to reflect. Be sad and cry and let it all out. All that is there for you to do is sit with the pain. Accept it and start a new chapter, but continue carrying the moments and memories you have of her. I pray this transition won't bring you down. You always tell us to analyse and reflect in terms of understanding literary texts, but I think this applies in life situations too. I have something small for you, and I hope you don't mind if I bring it to your office. —Yasmeen*

> *Yasmeen had always been an animal lover and one of my brightest students. I had tweeted about the loss of Flake and she had reached out to me. I was touched by her gentleness, her approach, and more importantly, her desire to extend her care to me. Yasmeen's gift was a keychain with Flake's name engraved on it and the years 2004–2018. It was the keychain that I would carry with me every day, reminding me of Flake and the love that surrounds my love for her. It is Yasmeen who reminds me of who I am when I am a lost. It is Yasmeen who centres me in my "homeplace," my place as a teacher, and reminds me of self-reflexivity. She writes this message out of a place of love and I receive it with love. ("Narrative Reflections on Losing a Companion Animal: In Memory of Flake")*

I have always negotiated the boundaries between respected professor and vulnerable human being. In shared vulnerabilities, I have found a third space, a space of belonging. I am extending these stories to you now. I used to think I was unique, but as I walked into the path of feminist theory and disability studies, I realised there was nothing original about my story. Yes, there are specific details that make up who I am and my experiences, but there are many features and events that affect many women of my time. These women are my friends, students, neighbours, friends of friends, circles upon circles, layered accounts that bleed into each other on this canvas. I have tried not to speak for anyone other than myself, to tell only my story, but inevitably, I have strayed into miniature narratives that have overlapped and blended with mine. Each story and each moment results from compounding stories, moments, and conversations. It is all organic, filled with movement, filled with possibilities, transitions, and gradually these experiences, these moments where we meet, become the bridge of the narrative we tell together.

I have listened to others' stories and have taken them in, allowing myself the privilege of vulnerability. Through vulnerabilities exposed and tended to, telling stories becomes the site of meeting, the place we turn to. I published stories, collections of poetry, academic articles, autoethnographies, and many pieces which were all an attempt at narrating the silenced body. I wanted to trouble the relationship between academia, society, women's bodies, and what we expect out of these categories. Every time I was invited to speak at a conference or a writers' workshop, I was met with surprise. People were always taken aback that I had chosen to write my body's stories, that I had broken the silence society expects Arab women not to break. But this wasn't all me. I don't sit there and tell them it was all the feminist and disability scholars that carried me through. I am indebted to Audre Lorde's work, Nancy

Mairs's exploration of her body and academic identity, Arthur Frank's examination of illness narratives, Sara Ahmed's *Living a Feminist Life* and her insistence on staying a student, on carrying companion texts with us in our survival toolbox. I have carried these scholars and authors with me as my companion texts on this journey. But my narrative is still emerging, it is unfinished, and I don't know if it ever will finish—unless I die. Even then, illness narratives will re-emerge for others and different women will chronicle their own journeys. If I don't write this narrative now, if you hadn't convinced me to write, I would die. I need to write; this is the only movement I can afford now. The words will move to you, into you, and into others.

Narrating is part of survival. Those who survive know that there is a story to tell, and another to edit, recreate, and pass on. But those who survive also know that there is no ultimate path to healing, to full recovery, that you don't always come back to where you started, that we don't come full circle. Those who tell stories tell them as they occupy more than one space, reflecting on a past, speaking in the present moment, and anticipating a future. I am reminded of feminist scholar Gloria Anzaldúa, Chicana feminist, who speaks of the "mestiza" as being one who occupies more than one space, culture, and language. To survive, one must find solace in a third space of belonging. You are already outside of the dominant narrative, outside the margins, away from the centre.

Throughout the years, I realised that no matter how hard I tried to survive through documentation, I cannot relive past moments. I cannot conjure the parts of my life I have lost and the parts of me I want back. I remember re-learning how to walk. That was an art. The art of losing, the art of mastering it again.

The fear that came with trying again, placing one foot before the other, recognising my toes were mine. My feet had to do their job. I had never imagined I would forget the mechanics of walking. Looking up, holding on to safe and sturdy arms, step by step. And then finally, I was finding my feet, my rhythm, and Mama was there, waiting. Watching, wanting to see if I would make it without falling.

But how do we confront loss after loss? Write it. "Write it" is what poet Elizabeth Bishop tells us. I know the poem "One Art" like I know my mother's voice so well, always ringing in my ears:

> *The art of losing isn't hard to master;*
> *so many things seem filled with the intent*
> *to be lost that their loss is no disaster.*
>
> *Lose something every day. Accept the fluster*
> *of lost door keys, the hour badly spent.*
> *The art of losing isn't hard to master. . . .*
>
> *I lost two cities, lovely ones. And, vaster,*
> *some realms I owned, two rivers, a continent.*
> *I miss them, but it wasn't a disaster.*
>
> *—Even losing you (the joking voice, a gesture*
> *I love) I shan't have lied. It's evident*
> *the art of losing's not too hard to master*
> *though it may look like (Write it!) like disaster.*
>   *("One Art")*

Chapter R of Four

If illness is to be feared and has contagion as its constant shadow, then may this book be contagious.

If I can share my memories, may you share them with others, if I can tell you a story, may you share it with others. If I can touch you, I touch myself, if I can reach you, then I can reach myself, recover a part that has been buried through years of silence and shame. My academic background plays a role in the fashioning of this book, but by no means does it constitute a critical study—this is at most a response to various stimuli in the "grand" narrative of life. I couldn't decide on a beginning, but ended up in the middle of the narrative, and now I can't decide on an end. My mother has always said that we all have a vehicle in life. You might have a small car, a bicycle, a motorcycle, or a luxurious car. The vehicle takes you places on your journey, but it also hinders you. It may stop, break down, falter, or need you to pull over for a while. Each chapter pulls over, it stops at parts of the narrative. I have had a total of three car accidents so far, each time coming so close to death.

When I taught writing classes, I urged students to think of a beginning, middle, and end. Writing offers an illusionary structure to narrative. But in illness there is no apparent structure. Days and experiences of pain overlap. It becomes hard to locate a clear beginning. When doctors ask, "When did the pain start?" we cannot remember an exact date, a precise moment. When you start feeling better, you are not sure whether it was day seven or day ten or day fourteen. Somewhere in the middle, somewhere in-between there was a change. The ending is not what I am interested in. The outcome of recovery is what society wants to hear, but recovery is not the ending I pursue, neither in my life nor my writing. What I am interested in is the healing of the soul from the traumas that are accumulated over the years of the body being damaged. Damage is always possible.

Imam Al-Shafi'i once said, "Health is a crown that the healthy wear, but only the sick can see it." Health is often seen as a privilege, and sick bodies as oppressed. I would like to think that even with losing the crown, I am finding new ways of being and becoming, a status among the margins, living between boundaries of illness and wellness, constantly finding new definitions of embodiment and living. I have to learn to exist in this grey area and resist falling into dualistic thinking of good/bad, healthy/sick, successful/failure. Healthy people want to believe that illness and disability doesn't just happen. There are many ways to think about this. Some people believe that righteous and good people don't just get sick. Some healers believe it is karma. Others believe it is a test of your faith. Others think of illness as a corporeal punishment that is either inflicted by God or by your own ill-doings and weaknesses. Healthy people need to believe these myths in order to keep disease at bay, to stay far away, to believe that illness cannot touch them if they stay good. Your thoughts control your life, you shouldn't be sick, you should find a way out, you should exercise, you were a bad teenager, you hurt too many people in a past life, you must have offended God; these are some of my favourite accusations. Accusing the ill person for failing to behave, failing to be strong enough, successful enough, failing to swim, leaves the healthy and able-bodied feeling safe and secure. They are at shore, sunbathing, while the rest of us are trying not to drown. But the possibility of the tide coming in and covering the edge of the shore, or even a tsunami overwhelming the beach, is always there. You can't always stay protected and distant. I have been in both spaces. I have been outside and in the water. I now know that I will exist here and there, and mostly there, head trying to stay above water, my deconditioned muscles paddling along, and my body's buoyancy reminding me that I am still here.

Afterword

Multiple sclerosis involves the body attacking the myelin sheath that surrounds and protects our nerve cells, rather like insulation on a live wire. As the sheath unravels, the signals travelling in the nerve cells become distorted, inefficient. And the unravelling and inflammation results in scars on the brain and throughout the nervous system all over the body. "Sclerosis" is derived from Greek, the abnormal hardening of tissue. I had stared many times at the magnetic resonance imaging (MRI) images that the neurologist would attempt to read and found myself utterly lost in translation. I couldn't see what he saw. I couldn't find myself anywhere in these images but I was fascinated that each scar had a different story to tell, a different path to interrupt, a different accent, and each scar appeared at a different time, yet no one could tell exactly when, which date, which year, during which season of the year. The scars accumulated over time and if you were to look inside my brain and spinal cord, you wouldn't find diary entries, or blog posts that describe me.

I have offered these snapshots from memories and diary entries. As with MS, these memories are fragmented, multiple, and have been written onto my body such that they are now a part of my thought process. They are the result of years of framing an illness narrative, a life-interrupted narrative, and one that captures the different angles of my kaleidoscope as I look inwards.

For more blog entries see:
www.drshahdalshammari.com

Glossary

Abaya: a full-length black outer garment worn by women

Aib: shameful, cultural taboo

Aish wa milh: an Egyptian saying meaning the sharing of food

Ala rasi Diktorah: a phrase showing respect

Al-janna tahta aqdam al-omahat: Heaven lies at the feet of mothers

Allah eysalmik: may God protect you

Ashahadu ana la ilahla ila Allah: there is no God but Allah

Asil: a term used to refer to lineage, race, where you come from, your origins

āstrāhaT mharib: a warrior's break from battle

Azrael: angel of death in Islam and Judaism

Azza: an Islamic ritual of empathy where respects are paid to the family of the deceased for up to three days after the burial

Dishdasha: a long robe with long sleeves

Ghutra: a piece of cloth that covers the head

Hadar: city dwellers

Ishra: to have history with someone, share a life with them

Khalas: enough

Ma afham englaizi: I don't understand English

Ma'a al-salamah: goodbye

Nabati poetry: Bedouin poetry with Bedouin dialect

Niqab: a veil covering all the face apart from the eyes

Sot almara'a 'awra: a woman's voice is taboo

Wasta: clout, getting something through favoritism

Ya'ateek al-afyah: may God grant you health/vigor

Acknowledgments

There are many people who have influenced my thinking and supported my journey to manifest this book. I don't trust that my memory will stand by my side in this futile attempt, but here goes. First, I am eternally grateful to Archna Sharma, my UK publisher, who took a chance on seeing this book develop and see the light. Archna believed that we could all relate to the experiences I have tried to share. Thank you for your patience and unwavering faith in me.

To Feminist Press, my ideal home for this book in the US, a press I have followed ever since I was an undergraduate studying literature. A very special thank you to Margot Atwell, executive director and publisher of Feminist Press. Thank you for championing this book and for being an ally to those of us who need someone like you at the forefront of all difficult spaces.

A quick thank you to my students, who gave my life a different meaning. You have unknowingly left your mark on every page of this book.

To my family and friends: thank you for sharing my happiness in seeing this book emerge from a pile of diary entries, memories, and silence.

To Abrar, my sister, for her courage and lifelong friendship. To my baby sister, Noorah, for her rebelliousness.

To Fadwa, who insisted that I finish this book after I abandoned it many times.

Finally, thank you to Abeer, my mother, who has never stopped fighting for my life. Without you, I wouldn't have found my way.

Works Cited and Consulted

Ahmed, Sara. *Living a Feminist Life*. Durham, NC: Duke University Press, 2017.

Alshammari, Shahd. "Narrative Reflections on Losing a Companion Animal: In Memory of Flake." *Journal of Autoethnography* 1, no. 4 (2020): 378–87. University of California Press.

——. "Staying and Witnessing: Two Steps of Love." *Wordgathering* 14, no. 2 (2020), https://wordgathering.com/vol14/issue2/essays/alshammari/. Permission to Reprint from *Wordgathering: A Journal of Disability Poetry and Literature*.

——. "Cartographically Speaking: Jisim, Jismain." *Wordgathering* 13, no. 3 (2019), https://wordgathering.com/past_issues/issue51/essays/alshammari.html. Permission to Reprint from *Wordgathering: A Journal of Disability Poetry and Literature*.

Bishop, Elizabeth. "One Art" from *POEMS* by Elizabeth Bishop. Copyright © 2011 by The Alice H. Methfessel Trust. Publisher's Note and compilation copyright © 2011 by Farrar, Straus and Giroux. Reprinted by Permission of Farrar, Straus and Giroux. All Rights Reserved.

Frank, Arthur W. *The Wounded Storyteller: Body, Illness, and Ethics*. Chicago: University of Chicago Press, 1995.

Mairs, Nancy. *Carnal Acts*. Boston: Beacon Press, 1990. Reprinted by Permission of Beacon Press, Boston.

Roy, Arundhati. *The God of Small Things*. New York: Random House, 1997.

Said, Edward W. *Reflections on Exile and Other Essays*. Cambridge: Harvard University Press, 2000.

Tamas, Sophie. "Biting the Tongue That Speaks You: (Re)writing Survivor Narratives." *International Review of Qualitative Research* 4, no. 4 (2012): 431–59.

———. "Writing and Righting Trauma: Troubling the Autoethnographic Voice." *Forum Qualitative Sozialforschung / Forum: Qualitative Social Research* 10, no. 1, art. 22 (2008), http://nbn-resolving. de/urn:nbn:de:0114-fqs0901220. Permission to Reprint from Sophie Tamas.

Woolf, Virginia. *Mrs. Dalloway*. London: Penguin Books, 2000.

———. *A Room of One's Own*. London: Penguin Books, 2004.

———. *On Being Ill with* Notes from Sick Rooms *by Julia Stephen* (Middletown, CT: Paris Press, 2012). Reprinted by Permission of The Society of Authors as the Literary Representative of the Estate of Virginia Woolf.

Blog posts from www.drshahdalshammari.com.